A TO Z of Style

A to Z of Style

Compiled by
Amy de la Haye

Illustrations by Emma Farrarons

V&A Publishing

First published by V&A Publishing, 2011
Victoria and Albert Museum
South Kensington
London SW7 2RL
www.vandabooks.com

ISBN 978 1 85177 652 8

10 9   8   7   6   5   4   3   2   1
2015 2014 2013 2012 2011

Design: Here (www.heredesign.co.uk)
Copy-editor: Sarah Drinkwater
Illustrations by Emma Farrarons
Printed in China

Introduction

'Fashion is not an inanimate object, and it is never at rest, a distinction it shares with life itself, of which it seems to be some special and significant manifestation.'
James Laver, V&A curator and historian of fashion imagery, 1937

The quotations and definitions cited and fully referenced within this 'quotationary' are drawn from non-fiction sources; mostly autobiographies by fashion designers and texts authored by their clients, fashion commentators and authorities on correct etiquette. The statements date from post 1850, the period which laid the foundations of today's global fashion industry, and they define fashion as it relates to women.

The criteria for inclusion were succinct word formations that, to modern sensibilities, were witty, audacious and sometimes shocking, or provided insight into specific items of fashion, eras passed or the dynamics of the industry. The emphasis is upon historical quotes, which provide intriguing glimpses into how women lived in the past, but also act as a comparison so we can evaluate contemporary circumstances. Certain eras predominate, notably those following wars, when guidance on how to conduct modern lives abounds.

The terminologies of a trade, like the reputation of those designers who did not form documents for future eyes, can become eclipsed with the passage of time. Like the objects they define, it is critical they should remain in circulation. I have thus provided definitions for terms that are lesser known today.

The charming illustrations, by Emma Farrarons, depict fashion objects that are now safeguarded for posterity in the V&A's magnificent collections.

Amy de la Haye
Professor of Dress History and Curatorship, Rootstein Hopkins Chair
London College of Fashion, University of the Arts London

How to use this book

A to Z of Style seeks to inspire, inform and amuse a broad audience, united by their fascination for fashion, style and etiquette, past and present.

The quotations have been drawn from a multiplicity of sources, some famous, others widely circulated and some obscure.

Where it has not been possible to date a quote to one year, the dates of its author are given. The designers are identified in relation to their place of work, or where they presented their shows, rather than their place of birth.

For further information, the references section starting on page 133 is organized by author: it provides all the page numbers for quotations from a particular person in the *A to Z of Style*, as well as further biographical information and the original sources.

Emma Farrarons's illustrations are inspired by the collections of the V&A Museum. You can find more details about the individual objects featured on page 130.

We hope that the *A to Z of Style* will be a useful resource for further research – and that it will inspire some thoughtful dressing.

A — AIGRETTE

The upright feathers from an egret (or heron) used to form or decorate millinery, fans and other fashion accessories. The term is sometimes used to describe hair or jewels that are arranged in a shape resembling feathers.

ACCESSORIES

'The less you can afford for your frocks, the more care you must take with your accessories.'
Christian Dior, Parisian fashion designer, 1954

'They are the signatures of your special tastes, clues to the type of woman you like being. Each is an idea in itself and you will quickly learn that you can't wear too many ideas at the same time.'
Claire McCardell, New York fashion designer, 1958

'The most important accessory for any woman is a full length mirror.'
Caroline Herrera, New York fashion designer, 2004

'My understanding is that the word "accessory" can also mean an "accomplice in crime" – the implication makes me hate accessories.'
Yohji Yamamoto, Paris-based fashion designer, 2010

AGE

'The full-blown rose is just as beautiful as the bud – the heart of the rose is not visible until the flower is full-blown – and the full-blown rose never attempts to look like the bud!'
Margaret Story, fashion and etiquette writer, 1924

'Nature gives you the face you have when you are twenty. Life shapes the face you have at thirty. But it is up to you to earn the face you have at fifty.'

Gabrielle 'Coco' Chanel, Parisian fashion designer, 1883–1971

'You can dress to suit yourself – and therefore your age – but this does not mean that you have to wear clothes that make you look old.'

Christian Dior, Parisian fashion designer, 1954

'At the most, all cosmetics can do is to give you back three or four years: and what good is that to anybody? You might just as well be chic and interesting.'

Hardy Amies, London fashion designer and royal dressmaker, 1954

AIGRETTE

'By the middle of 1912, we find complaints, in the more conservative journals, against the absurdity of high hats with bolt-upright trimmings which consisted of the single plume … intricate twists of ribbon supported on a wire, or of spikes of such upstanding flowers as hollyhocks. Sometimes a whirl of white lace was wired into a tall aigrette, and sometimes aigrettes themselves were used.'

James Laver, V&A curator and historian of fashion imagery, 1937

'A single consignment of 40,000 hummingbirds is common to supply aigrettes.'

C Willett Cunnington, fashion collector & historian, 1948

THE AMERICAN LOOK
(see also Sportswear, page 107)

Hattie Carnegie started her career in the 1920s and became one of America's most successful designers. Alongside her own designs, she imported models from Paris and translated these for the American market.

'She always also made up her own adaptations of their designs. And many American women came to feel that they were more likely to be satisfied with a dress if it was a Carnegie model, than if it were an exact duplicate of a striking novelty just launched on the Rue de la Paix.'

Beryl Williams, writer on American fashion, 1948

'For me it is American – what looks and feels like America. It's freedom, it's democracy, it's casualness, it's good health. Clothes can say all that.'

Claire McCardell, New York fashion designer, 1958

'American women won't wear thick tweeds: nor uncomfortable clothes at all. And they are quite right.'

Hardy Amies, London fashion designer and royal dressmaker, 1954

ARPETTE
The young woman who picks up the pins from the floor of the couture workroom.

B — BUTTON

An item made for the purpose of fastening clothing and occasionally used as decoration. Made from a variety of hard materials, it is usually round in shape and is pierced. A shank or loop enables it to be attached to the garment.

BELT

In the 1900s, waistbands were worn to accentuate the waist and, as dresses were made in two pieces, to cover the join between the bodice and skirt. It was not until the First World War (1914–18) that women wore belted garments as everyday dress.

'Very few people can afford to wear a sharply-defined ornamental waistband, although some of the embroidered bands worn with light gowns are so beautiful that it is difficult to resist their charms.'
Mrs Eric Pritchard, journalist and writer, 1902

'More often decreed by fashion than banished from it, a belt is the *gendarme* [police officer] of a woman's waistline.'
Genevieve Antoine Dariaux, Directrice at the House of Nina Ricci (Paris), 1964

BIAS CUT

'Maybe because everyone else made dresses that flowed in the same direction, I saw that if I turned the fabric on an angle … it gained elasticity.'
Madeleine Vionnet, Parisian fashion designer, 1876–1975

'The bias cut turns the fabric to water. It allows the fabric to speak.'
Roland Mouret, Parisian fashion designer, 1998

BLACK & THE LITTLE BLACK DRESS

'Women think of every colour, except the absence of colours. I have said that black had everything. White too. They have an absolute beauty. It is perfect harmony.'

Gabrielle 'Coco' Chanel, Parisian fashion designer, 1883–1971

'The Chanel "Ford" – the frock that all the world will wear.'

American Vogue, 1926

'Undoubtedly black is the smartest thing for town, particularly in the afternoon. However, since good black things are expensive and cheap black things look charity child-ish, black has become the uniform of the rich and chic, while the rest of us get by quite nicely on carefully calculated browns and greys and greens and wines.'

Margaretta Byers, fashion writer, 1939

'The violent accent of black makes it the most elegant colour.'

Christian Dior, Parisian couturier, 1905–57

'Functional: A simple black dress that costs more than $100. Understated: A simple black dress that costs more than $200. Nothing: A black dress that costs more than $300, as in "a little Nettie Rosenstein nothing."'

E. Merriam, writer on the fashion industry, 1960

'My earliest memory is of a black velvet dress. I must have been about nine years old.'
Gianni Versace, Milanese fashion designer, 1946–97

'The little black dress always looks better in white.'
Bill Blass, New York fashion designer, 2002

'Black is at the same time material, colour, shadow and light. It is neither happy, nor sad, but it is allure and elegance, perfect and necessary. It is as irresistible as the night.'
Christian Lacroix, Parisian fashion designer, 1951–

'Black is "an intellectual, contemporary colour."'
Yohji Yamamoto, Paris-based fashion designer, 1943–

'A panoply of associations attends achromatic black.'
Valerie Mendes, curator and fashion historian, 1999

BOUTIQUES

The term boutique was first used by the Paris couturiers in the 1920s, who introduced shops within their salons with accessories, perfume and ready-to-wear sportswear and sweaters.

'Dali dyed an enormous stuffed bear in shocking pink and put drawers in its stomach … Bettina borrowed it for the Boutique, and dressed it in an orchid satin coat and loaded it with jewels.'
Elsa Schiaparelli, Parisian fashion designer, 1954

'There was a time when clothes were a sure sign of a woman's social position and income group. Not now. Snobbery has gone out of fashion, and in our shops you will find duchesses jostling with typists to buy the same dress.'
Mary Quant, London fashion designer, 1965

'The boutique shopper is a modish magpie, in chic town black. She flits, not from branch to branch as does the common stores-shopper, but from boutique to boutique, picking out the pretty shining things and carrying them back to her boudoir.'

Alison Adburgham, Vogue editor, journalist and fashion historian, 1957

BOWS

'The most natural ornament of a dress because they are a natural way of closing and tying material.'

Christian Dior, Parisian fashion designer, 1954

BUSTLE

The bustle was introduced in 1868 to exaggerate a woman's posterior. Sometimes structured and made from steel, or otherwise fullness was created by using a pad that was held in place by a waistband. Fashionable until the early 1880s, it was revived (along with the crinoline) as part of the neo-Victorian trend of the late 1930s; by Yohji Yamamoto for autumn/winter 1986 and, more overtly, by Vivienne Westwood in her 'Café Society' collection for spring/summer 1994.

'The dress of 1875, with its bustle and tightly pulled-back skirt, was so tight that it was impossible for a fashionable lady to walk upstairs without assistance. The same predicament befell the wearers of the hobble skirt in 1914.'

Pearl (Polly) Binder, graphic artist and dress historian, 1953

BUTTON HOLE

A slit or loop through which to place a button.

BUTTONS

'It has been suggested that ... the practice may be connected with the desire to leave the right hand free in the case of the man, in order that he might hold his sword or implement, and the left hand free in the case of a woman. A woman, when buttoning up, would, it is supposed, grasp her attire with her right hand and push it over to the left, leaving her left arm free to carry a child.'

J.C. Flugel, social psychologist, 1930

Paris, 1930s:

'The most incredible things were used, animals and feathers, caricatures and paperweights, chains, locks, clips, and lollipops. Some were of wood and others of plastic, but not one looked like what a button was supposed to look like.'

Elsa Schiaparelli, Parisian fashion designer, 1890–1973

'Sometimes one button, well placed, gives a better effect than an eruption of buttons.'

Christian Dior, Parisian fashion designer, 1954

'A button is not a useless ornament, and nothing devalues a dress as much as a button that cannot really be buttoned.'

Genevieve Antoine Dariaux, Directrice at the House of Nina Ricci (Paris), 1964

'If, as sometimes happens, a buttonhole keeps slipping off the button at a strategic spot on the bodice, twist a small rubber band under the button. It will be unnoticeable and the rubbery texture will adhere to the fabric, at least until you get home.'

Anne Fogarty, New York fashion designer, 1959

C — CRINOLINE

The French word *crin* refers to coarse hair – usually from a horse – which was woven to make heavy petticoats for women to wear beneath a long skirt to create a full silhouette. In 1856, a lightweight flexible structure that resembled a cage was manufactured in steel, and named the crinoline. Satirical cartoonists depicted this structure as imprisoning women. The crinoline was revived in the late 1930s and then for spring/summer 1985 with Vivienne Westwood's 'mini-crini'.

CASHMERE

'The cashmere goat, aloof, remote is apt to be elusive, he little knows how far that goes, to making him exclusive.'
Jaeger's Natural History, 1930s

CHIC

'If you cannot be chic, at any rate you need never be aggressive, and above all you need not aim at being aggressively smart.'
Mrs Eric Pritchard, journalist and writer, 1902

'There is no word in English for chic. Why should there be? Everything chic is, by legend, French.'
Elizabeth Hawes, New York fashion designer and writer, 1938

'The essence of casual refinement, chic is a little less studied than elegance and a little more intellectual.'
Genevieve Antoine Dariaux, Directrice at the House of Nina Ricci (Paris), 1964

A TEST ON 'CHIC-OLOGY'

1. Do you wear patent leather shoes in the winter?

2. For a gala evening, would you wear false eyelashes?

3. With a limited fur budget, would you splurge on a lush fur lining rather than an inexpensive fur coat?

4. To a summer formal, would you wear a satin coat over a cotton dress?

5. Do you sometimes build an ensemble around an unusual accessory?

6. Would you wear a tweed dress to a cocktail party?

7. If you had only one piece of real jewellery, would you wear it in solitary splendour rather than combine it with imitation?

8. When the new hat style comes out, do you change your hairstyle to suit them?

9. Would you wear a cocktail length dress to a formal ball?

10. Would you wear a velvet hat with a summer cotton?

> 'To my way of thinking – and keep in mind that chic is purely personal – the chic answer to all ten questions is, Yes.'
> *Anne Fogarty, New York fashion designer, 1959*

CLIENTS

'There are only two kinds of women in the world of clothing. One buys her clothes made-to-order, the other buys her clothes ready-made.'

Elizabeth Hawes, New York fashion designer and writer, 1938

'Customers and Criminals

There are all sorts of customers … the manner in which they greet me classifies them in my mind immediately. There are those who wish to prove to themselves that I am a lower form of humanity. They say nothing to me, then try hard not to acknowledge my existence. The aggressively democratic: these shake hands with me as they pass, but carefully look the other way as they do so. Normal greeting and reasonable good manners. Hugs, kisses and passionate joy at seeing me. Class number one get charged 10,000 francs extra, because on top of their bad manners they are usually bargainers.'

Ginnette Spanier, Directrice of the House of Balmain, 1959

COLLAR

'The collar of a garment, along with the set of the sleeves, is the most delicate point of its construction, and it is here that two apparently identical garments immediately betray their difference in quality and price.'

Genevieve Antione Dariaux, Directrice at the House of Nina Ricci (Paris), 1964

COLOUR, PATTERN AND SURFACE

In 1857, synthetic aniline dyes became available which facilitated brighter colours that did not fade as fast as natural dyes.

'We wear forms – we see forms – we like and dislike forms, places, shades and colours. Form and fashion go hand and hand, links of the same harmonious chain creating all the outward life we live.'

George P. Fox, fashion writer, 1872

1883:

'It was observed in '83 that "in ballrooms lighted with the new electric light, the aesthetic shades of colour lose their effect and something more pronounced is necessary." The startling colour combinations of the eighties and nineties may well have been experiments, as it were, to discover colour schemes appropriate to the new form of illumination (which was much yellower in tone than the modern electric light).'

C Willett Cunnington, fashion collector & historian, 1948

'Purple is declared the colour of power. According to that, a woman can get what she goes after in violet shades.'

Margaretta Byers, fashion writer, 1939

On combining fabric:

'Let's divide our materials into four groups: sports, street, matinee or cocktail and evening; and agree to make combinations only within these groups.'

Margaretta Byers, fashion writer, 1939

'I believe in mixing patterns and colours wildly. So far as I am concerned, spots go with stripes and checks.'

Mary Quant, London fashion designer, 1934–

On Missoni, the Italian fashion company known for knitwear:

'To cover one's body with the sand of the Sahara, with the frosting flowers of a Viennese cake, with Persian miniatures, with playing cards, or with mosaics from Ravenna, the titles of San Marco, with butterflies, postcards, wristwatches, Victorian toys? The visual character of fashion by Missoni – symbols, colours, materials, forms – such an integral part of a unique style, has represented one of the most meaningful stimuli during the course of my career as a writer.'

Anna Piaggi, Italian fashion writer and style icon, 1994

'I always say to women that when you're out at night and in a sea of men in dark suits, wear red or white and you'll be noticed.'

Bill Blass, New York fashion designer, 2002

DIANA VREELAND ON COLOUR

'All my life, I've pursued the perfect red. I can never get painters to mix it for me. It's exactly as if I'd said, "I want rococo with a spot of Gothic in it and a bit of Buddhist temple" – They have no idea what I'm talking about. About the best red is to copy the colour of a child's cap in any Renaissance portrait.'

_____

'And though it's so *vieux jeu* [old hat] I can hardly bear to repeat it – pink is the navy blue of India.'

_____

'In Paris, Molyneux had a salon painted and carpeted in another perfect shade of grey. All his *vendeuses* [sales women] wore crêpe de chine dresses of the exact same colour. Everything was gray so that the clothes he was showing would stand out. You saw nothing except the clothes he showed.'

_____

'At *Harpers Bazaar*, a story went round about me: apparently, I'd wanted a billiard-table green background for a picture. So the photographer went out and took the picture. I didn't like it. He went out and took it again. I didn't like it. "I asked for a billiard-table green!" I'm supposed to have said.

"But this is a billiard table, Mrs Vreeland", the photographer replied.

"My dear," I apparently said, "I meant the idea of billiard-table green, not a billiard table."'

Diana Vreeland, curator and editor of Harpers Bazaar and American Vogue, 1984

COSMETICS

'The Lips

From very ancient times, lemon has been a favourite means of promoting their redness: a slice of lemon or lime daily rubbed on the lips just to cause tingling, leaves them pleasantly red, provided they are not cracked.'

Cora Brown Potter, actress, 1908

'Some people seem to have an idea that the use of face powder is a most reprehensible habit; indeed, I have met with those who consider it almost criminal for a woman to dust a little powder on her face.'

'Myrene', anonymous beauty writer, 1900

On the use of 'paint and powder':

'Its danger lies in the tendency to cultivate an artificial ideal.'

J.C. Flugel, social psychologist, 1930

'The most beautiful make-up for a woman is passion.'

Yves Saint Laurent, Parisian fashion designer, 2002

COUNTRY CLOTHES

(see also the London Look and Britishness, page 78)

'What to wear at a smart country house

If you intend to walk with the guns, you must have a properly made tweed Norfolk coat and short skirt with regulation pockets, and sensible boots for tramping over heather and stubble.'

Mrs Eric Pritchard, journalist and writer, 1902

'Right in the Country

The sameness of country clothes: delightful to live in low heels, tweeds, casual sweaters and artless cottons for a few week's holiday, but death to glamour if these are your uniform wear day in and day out, all the year round.'

Ira Morris, designer and art editor, 1947

The show for the press party which launched the opening of Mary Quant's second boutique, in Knightsbridge, London (1957):

'We were showing knee-high cowboy boots worn with fantastically short skirts; high-waisted tweed tunic suits with tweed knickerbockers; Norfolk jackets trimmed lavishly with fox collars. Eyebrows went right up to the hairline when the first models appeared. One girl carried an enormous shotgun; another swung a dead pheasant triumphantly round her head. Perhaps too triumphantly because the poor thing, which we had bought from Harrods across the road, thawed out all over the newly painted walls; even over some of the journalists.'

Mary Quant, London fashion designer, 1965

CRINOLINE

1856:

'Science came to the rescue. Circular hoops were devised, of diminishing size, like the ribs of an airship, and when these were sewn into an underskirt it was possible to give the impression of an enormous number of petticoats without, in fact, wearing any petticoats at all. The first crinolines must have given an astonishing sense of freedom to those bold spirits who adopted them.'

James Laver, V&A curator and historian of fashion imagery, 1937

'It symbolized in concrete form that Woman was beginning to occupy larger spaces in the social world.'
C Willett Cunnington, fashion collector and historian, 1948

D — DRESS

Noun – a one-piece garment worn by women and girls. A collective term for clothes and used to describe the act of putting on clothes.

DESIGN AND THE CREATIVE IMPULSE

'Inspiration is unconscious, or perhaps subconscious. Who can say exactly what gives rise to the creative impulse? A lingering melody or the cloying scent of lilies may suggest a romantic mauve dress for a sentimental matron. A wax-white magnolia dancing in the moonlight is a debutante dancing at Hurlingham ... and a farmyard is redolent of sporting tweeds.'

Norman Hartnell, London fashion designer and royal dressmaker, 1901–79

'I am often asked, why, with so many personalities floating around, all fashion seems to move in the same direction at the same time. Some think the dressmakers are in cahoots. On the contrary, they seldom meet and don't get along when they do.'

Carmel Snow, American Vogue writer and editor of Harper's Bazaar, 1961

'All a designer can do is to anticipate a mood before realizing they are bored with what they have already got. It is simply a question of who gets bored first. Fortunately I am apt to get bored pretty quickly. Perhaps this is the essence of designing.'

Mary Quant, London designer, 1965

'I think fashion dies when it is taken too seriously. There's more to life than buying a new bag or a new dress. I design clothes, produce them and sell them but I'm very aware that you can't take them home to bed with you and make love to them … clothes come pretty far down on my list of priorities.'

Perry Ellis, New York fashion designer, 1978

'This is a job of extreme precision and every piece of pattern has to fit each other to the exact millimetre. Every line has to flow properly throughout. Every measurement needed for making must be marked. Every grain line for cutting must be clear. A flat pattern has established seam measurements which run throughout each type of cloth or skin.'

Jean Muir, London fashion designer, 1981

'Creativity is not something that can be calculated.'

Rei Kawakubo, Paris-based fashion designer, 1997

DIET AND BODY

(see also Models and Mannequins, page 84)

'Nothing is more beautiful than the freedom of the body.'

Gabrielle 'Coco' Chanel, Parisian fashion designer, 1883–1971

'Women are pathologically aware of themselves – or rather, not of themselves, but of an inherently wrong conception of themselves. We are in an intensely self-conscious generation in a self-conscious civilization.'

Margaret Kornitzer, writer on family life, adoption and women, 1932

'If you wish to minimize too lush curves, avoid lustrous fabrics like the plague.'

Margaretta Byers, fashion writer, 1939

'Never fit the dress to the body, but train the body to fit the dress.'

Elsa Schiaparelli, Parisian fashion designer, 1954

'No sensible person admires a lovely figure that has been attained and retained by such rigorous dieting that the digestion is spoilt and the nervous system troubled. The figure may be lovely but there will be lines on the face, headaches, strain and a general malaise that will spoil the enjoyment of the sufferer.'

Betty Page, writer on the fashion industry and etiquette, 1954

'In short, the female body consists of a series of sterilized zones, which are those exposed by the fashion which is just going out, and an erogenous zone, which will be the point of interest for the fashion which is just coming in. The erogenous zone is always shifting, and it is the business of fashion to pursue it, without ever actually catching it up. It is obvious that if you really catch it up you are immediately arrested for indecent exposure. If you almost catch it up, you are celebrated as a leader of fashion.'

James Laver, V&A curator and historian of fashion imagery, 1937

On Biba's clients who:

'Were the post-war babies who had been deprived of nourishing protein in childhood and grew up beautiful skinny people. A designer's dream.'

Barbara Hulanicki, London fashion designer, 1983

Women's Wear Daily interview with supermodel Kate Moss:

'WWD: Do you have a motto?

KM: There are loads. There's "Nothing tastes as good as skinny feels." That's one of them. You try and remember, but it never works.'

Kate Moss, supermodel, 2009

DIRECTRICE

'Basically I would say the Directrice is responsible for every human problem throughout the part of the firm which the public can see.'

Ginnette Spanier, Directrice of the House of Balmain, 1959

DISCRETION

'Discretion, a sort of refined good taste, is very often a synonym for elegance, and until 8pm it should be your principal objective. But discretion should never be confused with drabness.'

Genevieve Antoine Dariaux, Directrice at the House of Nina Ricci (Paris), 1964

DRESSES

'Be on good terms with your clothes; in fact, quarrel sooner with your best friend than with your best frock.'

Mrs Eric Pritchard, journalist and writer, 1902

'A ball gown is your dream, and it must make you dream. Wearing a beautiful ball gown, you become a real woman, all femininity and daintiness and sweetness.'

Christian Dior, Parisian fashion designer, 1954

'Dresses are much better than a psychiatrist.'

Millicent Hearst, socialite and philanthropist wife of media tycoon Randolph, 1882–1974

'A dress is a fleeting architecture destined to ennoble the feminine body's proportions.'

Christian Dior, Parisian fashion designer, 1954

'You should have seen Balenciaga's violets. He was the greatest dressmaker who ever lived. Those were the days when people dressed for dinner, and I mean dressed – not just changed their clothes. If a woman came in a Balenciaga dress, no other woman in the room existed.'

Diana Vreeland, editor of Harpers Bazaar, Vogue and curator, 1984

'Nowadays it is not unusual to see several identical dresses at the same party and the girls love it. You can see them huddling together, delighted at the confirmation of their own good taste.'

Mary Quant, London fashion designer, 1965

E — ELEGANCE

A term usually, although not exclusively, used to describe women who possess a distinctive personal style and dignified demeanor, which transcends fashion, time, social position and wealth. While it eludes precise definition, it is instantly recognisable and most desirable.

ECCENTRICITY AND INDIVIDUALITY

'I know many intellectual and interesting women who look quite their worst when bedizened with diamonds and other gems, but these are the very women who can invest quaint, old-world ornaments with mystery and meaning.'

Mrs Eric Pritchard, journalist and writer, 1902

'Eccentricity is a caricature of originality, for originality is beneficial to fashion, whilst eccentricity contributes nothing at all ... the eccentric woman doesn't at all wish to be imitated, but only to make herself conspicuous.'

Genevieve Antoine Dariaux, Directrice at the House of Nina Ricci (Paris), 1964

'Why not be oneself? That is the whole secret of a successful appearance. If one is a greyhound, why try to look like a Pekinese?'

Dame Edith Sitwell, poet, writer and critic, 1887–1964

ELEGANCE

'Elegance must be the right combination of distinction, naturalness, care and simplicity.

Outside this, believe me, there is no elegance. Only pretension.'

Christian Dior, Parisian fashion designer, 1954

'Elegance is good taste plus a dash of daring.'

Carmel Snow, American Vogue writer and editor of Harpers Bazaar, 1961

'What is Elegance? It is a sort of harmony that rather resembles beauty with the difference that the latter is more often a gift of nature and the former the result of art. The origin of elegance is easily traced. It springs and develops from the habits of a civilized culture. The word comes from the Latin *eligere*, which means "select".'

Genevieve Antoine Dariaux, Directrice of the House of Nina Ricci (Paris), 1964

'Fashion is a passing thing – a thing of fancy, fantasy and feeling. Elegance is innate.'

Diana Vreeland, curator and editor of Harpers Bazaar and American Vogue, 1903–89

'Elegance is a dress too stunning to dare wear it twice.'

Yves Saint Laurent, Parisian fashion designer, 1936–2008

'Some women have a great deal of character and incredible charm, merely due to their intelligence, the way they speak and move or react. And that is worth all the elegance in the world.'

Valentino, Milanese fashion designer, 2008

EMBROIDERY

Decorative needlework, undertaken by hand or machine, using thread and needle to stitch into fabric.

'The adjective which automatically comes to mind when one speaks of embroidery is "sumptuous" – and well it might, for a dress that is embroidered all over can easily be as costly as a mink coat or a respectable large jewel.'

Genevieve Antoine Dariaux, Directrice of the House of Nina Ricci (Paris), 1964

'Embroidery is to haute couture what fireworks are to the 14th of July.'

François Lesage, head of celebrated embroiderers, the House of Lesage, 1929

ETIQUETTE

'The true meaning of etiquette can hardly be described in dictionary parlance: it embraces the whole gamut of good manners, good breeding, and true politeness.'

Manners and Rules of Good Society or Solecisms to be Avoided, 1893

'The word – an Anglo-Norman one – originally specified the ticket tied to the necks of bags or affixed to bundles to denote their contents. A bag or bundle thus ticketed passed unchallenged.'

Manners of Modern Society, 1877

christian Dior

F — FAN

A hand-held device used for cooling and/or flirting (historically, there existed a language which could be conveyed by particular movements). It comprises either a rigid or folding structure made in a variety of materials, which are often intricately decorated by incision and applied work. The first folding fans appeared in Japan in the seventh century, and then fans became fashionable in Europe and America from the late sixteenth century until the early twentieth century.

From the late 18th century:

'"Fanology" enabled two people to carry on a conversation with each other in secret by means of an elaborate secret fan code.'

Pearl (Polly) Binder, graphic artist and dress historian, 1953

'Regardless of the climate, the fan is chiefly an accessory of the toilet, affording an excuse for graceful movements under the pretext of agitating the air to refresh it. This flexible curtain, in turn, discloses all that is apparently hidden, conceals all that is apparently exposed.'

Charles Blanc, art critic, 1881

'The fad of carrying fans has put into women's hands an alluring weapon.'

Margaret Story, fashion and etiquette writer, 1924

FANCY BALLS

'A fancy dress ball allows of plenty of choice of dress ... but a ball costume must be kept strictly to one particular period of costume ... Yet another kind of fancy ball is a *bal poudré*. Here the guests are free to appear in ordinary evening dress, but with powdered hair ... The Calico Ball is a fancy ball at which the dresses are made of calico.'

Modern Etiquette in Private and Public, 1891

FASHION

'The current popular custom or style, esp. in dress or social conduct ... manner or style of doing something.'

Oxford English Dictionary, 1991

'Fashion is and has been and will be, through all ages, the outward form through which the mind speaks to the material universe.'

George P. Fox, writer on the influence of fashion, 1872

'No fashion has ever been driven out by convincing anybody that it was impractical and inconvenient.'

James Laver, V&A curator and historian of fashion imagery, 1937

'Fashion is that horrid little man with an evil eye who tells you that your last winter's coat may be in perfect physical condition, but you can't wear it. You can't wear it because it has a belt and this year "we are not showing belts."'

Elizabeth Hawes, New York fashion designer and writer 1938

'Fashion is in the air, it is borne on the wind, you can sense it, you can breathe it, it's in the sky and on the highway, it's everywhere, it has to do with ideas, with social mores, with events.'

Gabrielle 'Coco' Chanel, Parisian fashion designer, late 1940s

'Perhaps those who are claimed by fashion, rather than those who follow it, are the true exponents of the art of living.'

Cecil Beaton, writer, photographer, illustrator and costume designer, 1954

'Some people have it without knowing it – some people know it without having it.'

Claire McCardell, New York fashion designer, 1956

See page 84 for more on mannequins.

'I am well aware that most people think it is an exaggeration to place the art of fashion – this thing that vanishes with the season that inspired it – on a level with other arts. But isn't its very transience part of its aesthetic value?'

Celia Bertin, mannequin, 1956

'The most successful fashion wears itself out the quickest, because it is over-imitated and over-propagated.'

Christian Dior, Parisian fashion designer, 1957

'If you must be a slave to something, make it Scrabble or knitting or casserole cookery. Anything but fashion, where you must be the mistress of your fate.'

Anne Fogarty, New York fashion designer, 1959

'We in America accept fashion the way we accept electricity – as something that we can turn on and off and that is always available.'

Bettina Ballard, editor of French and American Vogue, 1960

'Like any other game, it follows certain rules and must be played with a limited number of pieces.'

Madge Garland, editor of Vogue and founding Professor of the Royal College of Art's fashion department, 1962

'The world is hooked on fashion. Why? Because it is correct for the time. Fashion is the perfect expression of the economic and social hour. Fashion is never wrong. Fashion is the projection of invention for the time. Listen to the music.
Watch the drab or gay colours as they come and go.

Invention is fashion because it is what the world needs.'

Diana Vreeland, curator and editor of Harpers Bazaar and American Vogue, 1975

'It's a big mistake to intellectualize fashion. Fashion is for the eye, not for the head, unless it's a tiara.'

Caroline Herrera, American designer, 2004

'Isn't the ultimate goal achieved if the person who has it on is having a nice time? That's all that matters when you are talking about something as silly as clothes. It's how you feel. Dressing or designing is really about understanding your goal in the outcome of an outfit.'

Todd Oldham, American fashion designer, 1986

'If fashion is clothes, then it is not indispensable. But if fashion is a way of looking at our daily lives, then it is very important indeed.'

Yohji Yamamoto, Paris-based fashion designer, 1943–

'Fashion has a reason "to be" because in fashion you can find new kinds of expressions about human beings.'

Ann Demeulemeester, Belgian fashion designer, 1959–

'Fashion, with its affinity for transformation, can act out instability and loss but it can also, and equally, stake out the terrain of "becoming" – new social and sexual identities, masquerade and performativity.'

Caroline Evans, fashion historian and critic, 2003

FEATHERS

Feathers were used to ornament men's dress from the 13th century, but were not used extensively for women's fashion until the 18th century. From 1918, various international treaties were agreed to avoid the use of feathers in fashion to prevent the extinction of certain birds.

'Feathers are lovely on a bird and glamorous on a hat, but they must be used with great discrimination.'

Christian Dior, Parisian fashion designer, 1954

'The feathers of last season have moulted away; no osprey, even for Ascot. But less plumage, more bloomage: never since those old Edwardian summers has there been such a fair flowering.'

Alison Adburgham, journalist and fashion historian, 1956

The interior of Biba, 1969:

'Ostrich feathers dyed in different colours replaced flowers as decoration.'

Barbara Hulanicki, London designer, 1983

FEET

'There is no portion of our bodies so branded for our sins as our poor feet ... Well if we must deform them, the pointed Watteau shoe, with its slender heel, is very pretty.'

Mrs H.R. Haweis, writer on fashion and interiors, 1878

FITTER

A fitter works with the vendeuse and her client (At Balmain there were eleven workrooms, with the Directrice managing their workload).

'In the workrooms, the fitter is supreme. But it is the business of the Directrice to allot the work to the different workrooms.'

Ginnette Spanier, Directrice of the House of Balmain, 1959

FLOWERS

Artificial flowers can be dated back to Egyptian times when flowers were fashioned from horn. The artificial flower making industry arose in Italy in the 18th century and by the mid-19th century had become a major ancillary trade to the couture houses in Paris.

'Next to the importance of wearing jewels and lace comes the wearing of flowers.'

Mrs Eric Pritchard, journalist and writer, 1902

'Flowers, "exquisite creatures" that they are, are beautiful always; but there are some cases where certain flowers, especially when worn by individuals, are more beautiful than others and a certain combination of flowers is more pleasing and expresses individuality than another.'

Mary Brooks-Picken, writer on making, interpreting and defining fashion, 1918

'Good artificial flowers are expensive but worth it: do not buy cheap ones; they look cheap and will defeat your object by belittling the rest of your outfit. One final warning: never wear either natural or artificial flowers unless they are perfectly fresh in appearance.'

Betty Page, fashion industry and etiquette writer, 1954

'Few elegant women wear real flower sprays these days, but since many men have not yet caught up with this and still present them – the polite thing to do is to pin it in and look pleased.'

Anne Edwards and Drusilla Dreyfus, fashion and etiquette writers, 1956

'Flowers for me are a great source of inspiration; I like to reproduce them on a dress, turning a woman into a bouquet.'

Valentino, Milanese fashion designer, 1932–

'Erdem Moralioğlu never met a flower he didn't like. For that matter, he never did a floral print we didn't like.'

Harper's Bazaar, 2010

FUR

'Character seems to be expressed to a great extent in fur. We all seem to know the woman who wears beaver, mole, skunk, fox, mink, sable and ermine.'

Mary Brooks-Picken, writer on making, interpreting and defining fashion, 1918

'The cult of mink still keeps pace with mink cultivation, yet, as even more mink farms start up in country after country, there must surely come a time when too many minks will be chasing too few film stars … it takes seventy to a hundred skins to make one mink coat. A hundred weasels! How many thousand, then, go to the Charity Ball?'

Alison Adburgham, Vogue editor, journalist and fashion historian, 1956

Ermine:

'The emblem of purity and of royalty.'

Christian Dior, Parisian fashion designer, 1954

From the 1980s, many international fashion designers and models pledged to never use or wear fur. In the 2000s, it was revived and in 2011 is once again a booming business. Stella McCartney has remained true to her principles and has never used fur or leather.

'The word "mink" in these curious days is apparently a symbol of all that is affluent, glamorous and desirable. To me it symbolizes affluence all right, but only the common sort.'

Noel Coward, playwright, composer and director, 1959

'It takes 40 dumb animals to make a fur coat, but only one to wear it.'

Greenpeace campaign, photographed by David Bailey, 1984

FURBELOW

'Furbelow. Furbeloe, plaited or ruffled, Trimming for Women's Petticoats, Scarves … metaphorically to overlay with ornaments.'

S. William Beck, The Drapers Journal writer, 1886

G — GLOVES

A protective covering for the hands with integral constructed finger forms (as opposed to mittens which are composed of a single sheath). Early cave paintings depict people wearing gloves: more recently, gloves have been extended in length to reach the upper arms to wear with a sleeveless gown.

GARDEN PARTIES

Garden parties are held from July to September.

'A garden party presents a favourable opportunity for the display of a pretty toilette, and simplicity should be the prevailing idea of a dress, whether it be a costly one or otherwise ... enjoy yourself and look as happy as possible. A stiff, constrained demeanour looks nowhere so bad as at a garden-party.'
Modern Etiquette in Public and Private, 1891

'In the 1930s, it was considered "the height of chic" to attend a formal garden party in a soft floating dress bedecked with a pattern of summer blooms, worn under a large shady straw "sailor" hat.'
Frances Hinchcliffe, former V&A Curator, 1988

GLAMOUR

'Glamour, a dated word today, was a Hollywood invention. It was the aura diffused by every famous film goddess, by Garbo, Dietrich, Hedy Lamarr or Myrna Loy; it was the setting of the spectacular movies of Paramount and Metro-Goldwyn-Mayer. Glamour implies not only beauty but wealth.'
Anne Scott-James, Picture Post journalist and fashion writer, 1913–2009

'The word "Glamour" has become so vulgarized by overuse that it has become the small change of advertising currency.'

Norman Hartnell, London fashion designer and royal dressmaker, 1955

GLOVES

'Gauntlet. An iron glove formerly thrown as a challenge; in modern phraseology signifying properly a long glove covering the wrist.'

S. William Beck, writer for The Draper's Record, 1886

'There is no doubt that the makers prefer to keep light shades in fashion, as they naturally sell at least three times as many pairs.'

Mrs Eric Pritchard, journalist and writer, 1902

'Glove etiquette is not all as complicated as many women believe. In general, gloves should always be worn in the street but never indoors, except at the theatre, at a formal reception, or a ball. They should always be removed when eating, even if it is no more than a cocktail canapé. But a lady never takes off her gloves to shake hands (unless, of course, they are very soiled gardening or riding gloves) and furthermore, she never needs to apologize for keeping them on.'

Genevieve Antoine Dariaux, Directrice at the House of Nina Ricci (Paris), 1964

'In town you cannot be dressed without gloves anymore than you can be dressed without a hat.'

Christian Dior, Parisian fashion designer, 1954

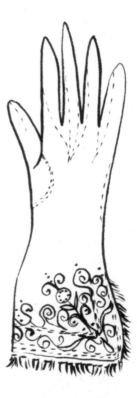

H — HANDBAGS

A bag carried in the hand and used by women since the eighteenth century (prior to this, separate pockets were worn around the waist to store small personal items). Today, there is a lucrative global economy for the latest designer 'It' bags, which come in a multiplicity of shapes, sizes, colours and materials.

HAIR AND FASHION

'A red-haired girl must accept the situation, and nerve herself to support the fierce glare which beats upon the auburn head. Let her turn her distinctiveness of appearance to account. Let her consider her hair as a central point to dress up to.'

Modern Etiquette in Public and Private, 1891.

HANDS

'The hand is a tell-tale member, and reveals all the character which the face tries to conceal.'

Modern Etiquette in Private and Public, 1891

HANDBAGS AND LUGGAGE

'The need for carrying about a number of small articles is one of the graver disadvantages of civilization.'

J.C. Flugel, social psychologist, 1930

'For sports: swagger bags
For suits or coats: envelope or pouch
For cocktail clothes: envelope with jewelled clasp
For evening clothes: small pouch or vanity.'

Margaretta Byers, fashion writer, 1939

'Your various pieces of luggage are useful servants, but they are very indiscreet ones, for they reveal your social situation even more clearly than your attire. They also reveal, according to the way in which they are packed, your character and habits.'

Genevieve Antoine Dariaux, Directrice at the House of Nina Ricci (Paris), 1964

New York, 1937:

'I've got cigarettes. I've got my lipstick, I've got my comb, I've got my powder, I've got my rouge, I've got my money. But what do I want with a bloody old handbag that one leaves in taxis and so on? It should all go in pockets. Real pockets, like a man has, for goodness sake.'

Diana Vreeland, curator and editor of Harpers Bazaar and American Vogue, 1984

'That women love bags is a fact for which the fashion business gives a collective hallelujah to the God of capitalism on a daily basis.'

Hadley Freeman, fashion journalist, 2008

HANDKERCHIEF

'There is considerable art in using this accessory of dress and comfort. Avoid extreme patterns, styles and colours. Never be without a handkerchief. Hold it freely in the hand, and do not roll it into a ball. Hold it by the centre, and let the corners form a fanlike expansion. Avoid using it too much. With some persons the habit becomes troublesome and unpleasant.'

Enquire Within Upon Everything, 1894

'Once in a while we see a little lady with "a saucy twinkle in her eye" from whose tailored suit pocket keeps a dainty little lace handkerchief. It is irresistible because we know she "knows better".'

Margaret Story, fashion and etiquette writer, 1924

'Handkerchiefs have always been a leading feminine weapon, a widely accepted cliché for attracting attention by fluttering or dropping to the floor ... tissues and hankies have a separate function. Tissues for utility; hankies for coquetry.'

Anne Fogarty, New York fashion designer, 1959

HAUTE COUTURE

Defined literally, haute couture means 'fine sewing'. Implicit in the term is a supreme quality of creative and innovative design and workmanship, with the provision of an individual made-to-measure service. In Paris, the *Chambre Syndicale de la Haute Couture Parisienne* was established in 1868 and issues strict criteria for designers seeking to use this legally protected term as it is much misused in other countries. In general, designers who provide a similar service are described as couturiers (as opposed to haute couturiers).

'Of all the translations of haute couture, I think I prefer "high sewing": it sounds rather like high finance or higher mathematics. What it really means, of course, is the making by hand of clothes of original design, bespoke by ladies. I say bespoken, because it is often forgotten that we execute orders: we do not sell clothes.'

Hardy Amies, London fashion designer and royal dressmaker, 1954

'A haute couture model is made up of any number of unexpected elements blown together like Cinderella's coach. Often it looks as if it had been both inspired and sewn by the fairies themselves, and one has a little constriction of the heart seeing it.'

Celia Bertin, mannequin, 1956

Paris, 1930s:

'I used to spend my day at fittings. I used to fit my nightgowns. I had three fittings in a nightgown. Can you imagine? People say: "What in the world were you doing that for?" Because that's the way you got a nightgown.'

Diana Vreeland, curator and editor of Harpers Bazaar and American Vogue, 1984

Paris, 1957:

'Motorcycle jackets in alligator, mink coats with sweater sleeves, turtleneck collars under finely cut flannel suits – those street inspirations all seemed

very inelegant to a lot of people sitting on the gilt chairs of a couture salon ... social structures were breaking up. The street had a new pride.'
Yves Saint Laurent, Parisian fashion designer, 1984

'Cost has no meaning in a couture dress. The result must simply be the ultimate aesthetic statement.'
Arnold Scaasi, American fashion designer, 1930–

'Haute couture is personal not only to the person wearing it but also to the person making it.'
Stephen Jones, London milliner, 1957–

HOSIERY

Covering for the leg and (usually) the foot, made of a knitted yarn. A generic term used to describe socks, stockings and tights.

'The bizarre in hosiery is never good style, being more suggestive of the chorus girl than the lady of fashion.'
Mrs Eric Pritchard, journalist and writer, 1902

'Most fastidious women insist upon the seam of the hose being directly in the centre of the calf of the leg and absolutely straight. The psychological effect of this care in putting the hose on straight is important in itself, for if we are careful about such little details we will be careful about the more important ones.'
Mary Brooks-Picken, writer on making, interpreting and defining fashion, 1918

I — IRONS AND IRONING

An iron is a heated instrument that is used to apply pressure to smooth a garment (ironing).

IMITATIONS

'An honest-to-goodness sheepskin coat is smarter than a Japanese mink. Good semi-precious jewellery is infinitely better than fake diamonds or rubies. Never compromise with quality. Dressing down is far smarter than trying to dress above your budget.'

Margaretta Byers, fashion writer, 1938

'Today the only people likely to take a snooty view of imitations are people who possess luxurious minks and jewels of their own on the Duchess-Maharanee level. And there always will be those with little sense of fashion who think it better form to wear a fox in diamond chips because it is genuine rather than an elegant Parisian fake.'

Anne Edwards and Drusilla Beyfus, fashion and etiquette writers, 1956

'The instinct of self-adornment is inherent in the human race.'

Nora M. Bickley, etiquette writer, 1956

INGÉNUE

A term traditionally used to refer to young – and by implication, innocent – women (often débutantes), and the pretty, romantic dresses suitable for them. The literal French translation is "unsophisticated".

INTERIORS AND FASHION

'The whole style of our modern furniture, as well as our modern dress, is largely due to these terrible white walls.'

Mrs H.R. Haweis, writer on fashion and interiors, 1878

INVITATIONS

'You cannot invite people to your house, however often you may have met them elsewhere, until you have first called upon them in a formal manner, and they have returned the visit. It is a kind of safeguard against any acquaintances which are thought to be undesirable. If you do not wish to continue to the friendship you discontinue to call.'

Manners of Modern Society, 1877

'Without ladies society cannot exist. All invitations (with the exception of those for dinner parties) are, therefore, sent out in the name of the mistress of the house, it being taken for granted that the gentleman will welcome his wife's guests, although his name does not figure in the invitation.'

Modern Etiquette in Private and Public, 1891

'A formal invitation may be written by hand, fully engraved, or partially engraved, and it is always worded in the third person.'

Vogue's Book of Etiquette and Good Manners, 1969

IRONS AND IRONING

'Travel irons cause more arguments than politics.'

Anne Fogarty, New York fashion design, 1959

'The woman who employs a self-heating iron does not have to consider saving steps, for instead of ironing near a hot stove or going back and forth to exchange a cold iron for a hot one, she can iron in one spot, and that a comfortable one.'

Laundering and Dry Cleaning, 1925

THE ITALIAN LOOK

Rome, summer 1947: 'Romans were dressing not for a city but for a resort. The streets were full of beautiful young women, all hatless, in sleeveless, pale-coloured linen dresses, bare legs and sandals.'

Audrey Withers, editor of British Vogue, 1905–2001

'It is the Marchesse Emilio Pucci who is Florentine fashion ... his printed silks and cottons, made into play clothes, have Tuscan designs and colourings ... from the cat in the courtyard to the sheep in the Palazzo, fashion is a little confusing in Florence. But, if there is a naïveté, there is also spontaneity, vitality, and individuality. And if, as Fabiani said in Rome, "Fashion is no longer in fashion", individuality must be sought and appreciated, or clothes will become just clothes.'

Alison Adburgham, journalist and fashion historian, 1957

'IT ISN'T DONE!'

'It isn't worth arranging to flaunt your latest model, and tell your friend you won't be changing.'

Betty Page, fashion industry and etiquette writer, 1954

J — JEWELLERY

A decorative (non-clothing) object used for adornment. The term is derived from jewel – a precious stone. Collectively it refers to items including rings, necklaces, brooches, bracelets, etc.

'A few slight ornaments are admissible at the breakfast table, such as earrings and brooches; but ornaments of a costlier kind, and set with brilliant stones, are utterly out of place. Diamonds in the morning always exhibit a trace of shoddyism. An elegant simplicity of dress, equally with unaffected manners, demands respect and will ever receive the admiration of persons of worth, taste, and culture.'

Daisy Eyebright, etiquette writer and contributor to the 'Woman's Page' of Country Gentleman, 1884

'There is something so terribly ordinary about a blaze of diamonds on a black frock, but the flashing of the same stones on a gown of white chiffon or velvet is truly wonderful.'

Mrs Eric Pritchard, journalist and writer, 1902

'It is not uncommon to see a young woman wearing, all at one time, a watch pinned to her blouse, several rings, from up to three bracelets, and a string of beads. Such a sight tells you that she is not practising the rule of elimination or applying the laws of harmonious dress to herself.'

Mary Brooks-Picken, writer on making, interpreting and designing fashion, 1918

'A very white earring on the lobe of a well-tanned ear delighted me.'

Gabrielle 'Coco' Chanel, Parisian fashion designer, 1883–1971

'There are three categories of jewellery: Real Jewellery, which includes precious stones and solid precious metals. Imitation Jewellery, which copies the settings and workmanship in semi-precious stones, filled or plated metals, and other synthetic means. Costume Jewellery, which is in a completely different category and is purely a fashion accessory, which changes its style along with other fashion trends.'

Anne Fogarty, New York fashion designer, 1959

JOURNALISTS

'Very few fashion journalists offer direct criticism: criticism is usually implied by omission – if they don't like you, they usually don't talk about you.'

Hardy Amies, London fashion designer and royal dressmaker, 1954

K — KNITWEAR

A clothing item which is made from a fabric comprising
interlocking loops, which is simultaneously constructed
and shaped. It can also be used to define knitted fabric
that has been cut and sewn.

KIMONO

A kimono (which translates literally as 'thing
to wear') is widely considered to be Japan's
indigenous dress. It is a flat, straight-cut, loose,
wide-sleeved, ankle-length robe, which is fastened
around the waist with a sash, called an *obi*. The
cut – and aspects of it, such as a 'kimono sleeve' –
has had an enduring influence upon international
fashion since Japan started to trade with Europe
and America from 1854.

'The coexistence of kimono and bias in 1920s and
1930s fashion was not entirely a historical accident.
Both forms of draping – the first enveloping and
the other disclosing and emphasizing – circulate
around the body, cylindrically, breaking zones of
front and back, establishing clothing as a gyrating
cylinder surrounding the wearer.'

*Richard Martin, associate curator, The Costume Institute
Collection, Metropolitan Museum of Art, 1995*

*See also page 71, Comme
des Garçons.*

'European-style couture involves giving three-
dimensional form to fabric by using cured lines and
darts to fit it to the body. But Japanese designers
were free from European couture methods, because
of the notion of the kimono in their minds.'

Akiko Fukai, curator of Kyoto Costume Institute, 2010

KINETIC FASHION

In 1925 couturier Lucien Lelong presented his kinétique silhouette at the International Exposition of Modern Industrial and Decorative Arts in Paris. His garments celebrated dynamism and motion, which were central to modernist preoccupations.

'I wanted my clothes to be constructed in such a way that their true shape would emerge in movement, not at rest.'

Lucien Lelong, Parisian couturier, 1889–1958

KNITWEAR AND KNITTING

'Chanel is master of her art and her art resides in jersey.'

British Vogue, 1916

Hollywood actress Lana Turner was called the 'sweater girl' after she wore a figure-hugging sweater in the 1937 film They Won't Forget.

'Knitting should be done thoughtfully. It should not be hurried. That is its charm to our generation, who live surrounded with a wild helter-skelter of speed. It is creative, and that is its supreme satisfaction.'

Mary Thomas, writer on knitwear, 1938

'One practical detail. As time goes on, would you like me to knit for the baby? I may tell you that I am the Knitting Queen ... ('a beautiful little knitter', I am told by experts. Why 'little'? I think it is an expression of approbation.) And no doubt you two will be wanting wraps and things. Blast the coupon system!'

Dame Edith Sitwell, poet, writer and critic, 1944

'Knitting is a most wonderful art. Though it has been known for centuries, we are often inclined to regard it as being quite a new invention. This is because during recent years, it has become extremely popular with both sexes in every class of society. Mother, father, all the children have their cardigans and pullovers. What a saving! What an insurance against a sudden chill!'

Mrs Robert Henrey, the autobiography writer Madeleine Henrey, 1956

Comme des Garçons' 'Lace' collection for autumn/winter 1982 featured black jumpers with holes that suggested shoddy workmanship, distress or moth attack. They were interpreted by the media as deconstructive or fulfilling the Japanese concept of wabi-sabi, which privileges the incomplete or faulty.

'The urge to knit is surely the most moral force in the world. Knitting is industrious, economical, virtuous, puritanical, and above all tranquillizing. Research would show that knitting wives never become nervous wrecks and that it is never knitting girls who break up happy homes. Conversely, it would be found that the Other Woman never knits.'

Alison Adburgham, Vogue editor, journalist and fashion historian, 1961

'When you are knitting socks and sweaters and scarves, you aren't just knitting. You are holding back time. You are preserving the simple unchanging act of handwork.'

Stephanie Pearl-McPhee, knitting writer, 2005

L — LINGERIE

A French word used to describe women's undergarments.

LABELS AND LOGOS

In 1922, Jean Patou became the first couturier to feature their monogram, declaring that a:

'Monogram will always add distinction to a very plain sweater.'

Jean Patou, Parisian fashion designer, 1880–1936

In 1988, Maison Martin Margiela opened in Paris. The company label has no words, just the numbers 1 to 23 printed in black onto white cotton, with the relevant collection identified by the number circled. The company communicates exclusively in the first person plural 'we'.

'We prefer that people react to a garment through their taste and own personal style and not their impression of the individual or group who created it.'

Maison Martin Margiela, company of Antwerp designer Martin Margiela, 1957–

'Most of all, logos reek of the worst kind of fashion victimhood.'

Hadley Freeman, fashion journalist, 2008

LAUNDERING CLOTHES

'The lengths to which our great grandmothers went to preserve their clothes seems nothing short of incredible in our labour-saving times. Dresses were carefully unpicked before washing, and sewn up again afterwards; while drying, lace was held in position by hundreds of pins … the housewife even made her own soap and blacking, and everybody learned how to clean silk dresses that could not be washed.'

Christina Walkley and Vanda Foster, curators and dress historians, 1978

Cleaning

In the 1850s it was the length of clothing and the environment that made outer clothes dirty, rather than the body, as women wore so many undergarments. Often just part of a garment – the hem for instance – would be spot cleaned, using dry (such as rubbing in and brushing off stale bread) or wet methods.

'Drying

When clothes are hung on the line quite wet, almost dripping in fact, the combined action of sun and air is one of the best bleaches known.'

Laundering and Dry Cleaning, 1925

LEATHER

Leather is the hide or skin of an animal (including some birds and fish) after it has been tanned or otherwise preserved. 'Hide' is the term used to refer to the leather obtained from larger animals such as cows, whilst 'skin' describes that from smaller beasts like goats and sheep. Suede is the French term for 'Sweden', which is where this velvety, and sometimes buttery soft, leather originated.

LEISURE WEAR

A peignoir is the French word for dressing gown. In English, it was used to refer to a flimsy, feminine dressing gown:

'(For at home) a gentlewoman need not be reminded that she should always be attired in a neat and becoming manner and that her dress ought to be adapted to the hours of the day. Such a woman will never appear at breakfast in a shabby peignoir, and then dress in the most stylish manner in street costume, or for evening visits.'

Daisy Eyebright, etiquette writer and contributor to the 'Woman's Page' of Country Gentleman, 1884

'Moralists would strive to teach us that they are a sign of the degeneracy of the age and that this easy comfortable dress points to free and easy manners.'

C.Willett Cunnington, fashion collector and historian, 1948

'Nothing is more conducive to a right beginning for the day's activity than donning a fresh, dainty house dress for breakfast. There is a barometric relativity between it and one's self respect and good humour.'

Margaret Story, fashion and etiquette writer, 1924

'At this very moment, the perfection of a tea gown may be realized by a combination of Japanese colouring, Grecian lines and French frivolity. Was there ever a time when fashions of all countries and periods were mingled with such excellent results?'

Mrs Eric Pritchard, journalist and writer, 1902

'Kitchen-Dinner Dress. For the cook who is the hostess. She cooks in the kitchen: you eat in the dinner there – but it's the best cooking you have ever had, and probably the best dress of a cook.'

Claire McCardell, New York fashion designer, 1956

LIGHTEN THE LOAD

'We might dispense with half our complicated folds, our whalebones, our scrunched toes, our immoveable arms, and many other miseries, and

Tea gowns were introduced in the 1870s. Usually made of a fragile material, these long gowns were worn at home from the late afternoon to early evening to provide respite from daytime corsetry and before dressing again for evening. A (married) woman could receive women guests for tea wearing her tea gown:

look less like mere blocks for showing off clothes and more like human beings: but we can't bear to let the housemaid or the crossing-sweeper think we have got sixpence in our pockets when it can be hung or piled on our backs, and we go about loaded like the celebrated camel who finally collapsed under a straw.'

Mrs H.R. Haweis, writer on fashion and interiors, 1878

LINGERIE

Bronze Age 2100 BCE: 'CRETE: corset stiffened with copper ribs to cinch waists of women and men.'

Berg's Encyclopaedia of World Dress and Fashion, 2010

'Under the crinoline, coloured knickerbockers were being worn in place of drawers … as petticoats were now objects for display, whether by design or accident, crinolines being treacherous in a breeze, these were trimmed almost as much as dresses with flounces, flutings and frillings.'

C.Willett Cunnington, fashion collector and historian, 1948

'There still exists, alas, a class of Englishwomen who consider dainty undergarments to be suggestive of evil, and insist that virtue can only be found in drab-coloured merino-wool combinations – thick, rough and high to the neck.'

Mrs Eric Pritchard, journalist and writer, 1902

'Even if she has the right amounts of fashion flair and cash to aspire to the lists of the best dressed, the woman with the wrong amount of bosom will never make it.'

Time, 1962

'It was still the age of the corset. I waged war upon it. The last representative of this abominated apparatus was called the Gache Sarraute. It divided its wearer into two distinct masses: on one side there was the bust and bosom, on the other, the whole behindward aspect, so that the lady looked as if she were hauling a trailer. It was almost a return to the bustle. Like all great revolutions, that one had been made in the name of Liberty – to give free play to the abdomen: it was equally in the name of Liberty that I proclaimed the fall of the corset and the adoption of the brassiere which, since then, has won the day.'

Paul Poiret, Parisian fashion designer, 1931

'Black and other dark-coloured stockings, even if they were of silk and partly transparent, had been usual up to the year 1926. In that year every woman's stockings suddenly became flesh coloured.'

James Laver, V&A curator and historian of fashion imagery, 1937

'The coquetry of corsetry, indeed, lies only in its language. Euphemistic and coy, at the slightest danger it scurries into French. And not always the right French.'

Alison Adburgham, Vogue editor, journalist and fashion historian, 1955

'The shortage of domestic help has certainly been an important factor in the present simplification of feminine lingerie and in the vogue for materials which are easy to launder, quick to dry, and require no ironing. But, alas, what is very practical is not always very elegant.'

Genevieve Antoine Dariaux, Directrice at Nina Ricci (Paris), 1964

Lingerie straps:

'A slipped strap can be the one false note in an otherwise perfect fashion composition.'

Anne Fogarty, New York fashion designer, 1959

Agent Provocateur opened in London in 1994:

'Here are pieces of material whose visual effectiveness is in inverse proportion to their size: miniature wisps of silk in pale blues and greens overlaid with ivory lace; delicate cotton camiknickers with saucy suspender attachments; stretchy black mini-corsets with a score of hooks-and-eyes round the back to drive boyfriends into paroxysms of frustration; hair-raising thongs in violet and plum; bras in floral strawberry-and-cream shades with tiny red rosebuds tucked in the middle.'

The Independent, 2002

THE LONDON LOOK AND BRITISHNESS

(see also Country Dress, page 27)

'There is enough mud and gloom in the British landscape without having to clothe the inhabitants in tones to match.'

Mrs Eric Pritchard, journalist and writer, 1902

'British fashion is self confident and fearless. It refuses to bow to commerce, thus generating a constant flow of new ideas while drawing in British heritage.'

Alexander McQueen, British fashion designer, 1969–2010

'I suffered from the unforgivable disadvantage of being English in England. There was only one thing to be done; to acquire a Parisian cache, however spurious.'

Norman Hartnell, London fashion designer and royal dressmaker, 1955

'I understand and admire the Englishwoman's attitude to dress, maddening though it may be at times. Just as our great country houses always look lived in and not museums, so our ladies refuse to look like fashion plates.'

Hardy Amies, London fashion designer and royal dressmaker, 1954

'Although Mr Macintosh must be counted as one of the greatest benefactors to the sodden inhabitants of the British Isles, habitual grumblers make discontented beneficiaries.'

Alison Adburgham, Vogue editor, journalist and fashion historian, 1955

'You have to have two sleeves and a hole to put the head in, which sometimes British designers forget.'

Donatella Versace, Milanese fashion designer, 2010

LUGGAGE

'Never take heavy luggage to a friend's house. If you want to take a good many dresses you should use a cane basket.'

Modern Etiquette in Private and Public, 1891

M — MILLINERY

Shaped headwear (as opposed to shawls and scarves) worn by women. A milliner was traditionally a term used to describe a maker of women's hats, as opposed to a hatter who made hats for men. Today some milliners also make men's hats.

MAKE DO AND MEND

A British Second World War campaign, headed by a fictitious Mrs Sew and Sew.

'It is an old-fashioned idea, that of keeping a "piece" box or bag, but it is one which economical women would do well to practise. Into these receptacles should go, in neat bundles, the cuttings of dresses, pieces of silk, velvet, lace, ribbon, trimmings, and buttons. The possibilities of the piece box in the hands of an economically minded and ingenious woman are endless.'

Gertrude Mason, writer on making and adapting clothes, 1945

'Now that combinations of materials of contrasting texture as well as of contrasting colour are in fashion, two well-worn garments can often be combined to make one good one ... a plain frock with worn or out-of-date sleeves can be turned into an attractive frock if allied with a little blouse ... a discarded wool dress joins forces with an old satin coat to produce the smart frock ... a useful bathrobe can be contrived from a discarded bathing wrap and an out-of-date swim suit.'

Gertrude Mason, writer on making and adapting clothes, 1945

'There comes a point in Making-Do and Mending when clothes and owner face each other with the realisation that this is the End.'

Ira Morris, designer and art editor, 1947

MIDINETTE

The women who do the stitching and sewing in a couture house.

MILLINERY

'And what shall we say of a fashionable bonnet, which is now perched so high above the formidable structures of hair which cover the crowns of our heads? It is merely a conglomeration of silk, illusion, feathers, blonde lace, flowers and ribbons, which is very becoming, however, to some faces, while to others it is a perfect fright.'

Daisy Eyebright, etiquette writer and contributor to the 'Woman's Page' of Country Gentleman, 1884

'A RECIPE FOR A BONNET.

On scraps of foundation, some fragments of lace,
A shower of French rosebuds to droop o'er the face,
Take ribbons and feathers, with crêpe and illusion,
And mix and derange them in graceful confusion;
Inveigle some fairy, out roaming for pleasure,
And beg the slight favor of taking her measure;
The length and breadth of her dear little pate –
And hasten a miniature frame to create;
Then pour, as above, the bright mixture upon it,
And lo! you possess "such a love of a bonnet!"'

Daisy Eyebright, etiquette writer and contributor to the 'Woman's Page' of Country Gentleman, 1884

'I think I may safely say, that economy, in the matter of headgear, is the last folly of the pauper.'
Mrs Eric Pritchard, journalist and writer, 1902

In 1938 the New York World Fair was staged. To mark the event, a time capsule was buried and the 'hat of the age' was requested – a draped silk emerald green and royal purple jersey turban with purple ostrich tips, held on with two jewelled fobs by Lilly Daché.

'The man-about-town, who wants his girl to look like a subtle siren, will like her best in a turban.'
Lilly Daché, New York milliner, 1946

'A hat can make you gay, serious, dignified, happy – or sometimes ugly, if you don't choose it well! A hat is the quintessence of femininity with all the frivolity this word contains! Women would be very silly not to take advantage of such an efficient weapon of coquetry.'
Christian Dior, Parisian fashion designer, 1954

'No two sides of a face are alike and it is surprising how few Englishwomen know which is their better profile. The French have long ago accepted this irregularity and a Frenchwoman seldom chooses a perfectly symmetrical hat or hairstyle. Dipping brims, one-sided trimming, even berets worn on one side are used to compliment the favourite profile.'
Betty Page, fashion industry and etiquette writer, 1954

'Hats are the dragonflies of the dress world.'
Alison Adburgham, Vogue editor, journalist and fashion historian, 1954

'The hat with no distinct idea is a helpless hat.'
Aage Thaarup, London milliner, 1956

'Personally I consider that a woman without a hat is not completely dressed. The fact that very young girls can get away with being hatless has encouraged their mothers to imitate them.'

Christian Dior, Parisian fashion designer, 1957

On the 1980s:

'Streets lost a lot of charm and wit when the hat disappeared.'

Christian Lacroix, Parisian fashion designer, 1951–

'You shouldn't ask, "Why do you wear a hat?" What you really should be asking is "Why are you not?" I can't imagine leaving the house without a hat. How can a look be complete without a hat? From a cap to a full-on fascinator, the hat is the accent, the exclamation mark, the finishing note that punctuates the whole look.'

John Galliano, London fashion designer, 2009

MINISKIRT

The introduction of the miniskirt has been credited to Mary Quant, Courrèges and to the model Jean Shrimpton who caused an outcry in 1965 when she attended the Melbourne Cup in Sydney wearing a dress that was 10cms above her knees.

MODELS AND MANNEQUINS

From the 1860s until the 1960s, the most exclusive were generally called 'mannequins' and the term 'model' was applied to describe a garment in a designer's

'Slowly the idea of a mannequin parade, which would be as entertaining to watch as a play, took shape in my mind. I would have glorious, goddess-like girls, who would walk to and fro dressed in my models, displaying them to the best advantage to an admiring audience of women ... not one of them

collection. The term
mannequin also refers to
the dressmaker's dummy
upon which clothes are
displayed.

weighed much under eleven stone, and several of
them were considerably more. They were "big girls"
with "fine figures", a compliment then, though it
has become the reverse now.'

*Lady Duff Gordon, the London fashion designer Lucile,
1932*

On Lucile's mannequin
Arjamand, 1918:

'The first of the really emaciated mannequins ever
to model fashionable clothes. She was so thin we
used to make cracks about stuffing cotton wool
between her vertebrae so that people wouldn't
think she was a skeleton.'

*Howard Greer, Lucile's assistant and Hollywood
costume designer, 1952*

'A good model can advance fashion by ten years.'

*Yves Saint Laurent, Parisian fashion designer,
1936–2008*

Twiggy (Lesley Hornby)
was 'The Face of the Year'
in 1966.

'We don't get out of bed for less than $10,000 a day.'

Linda Evangelista, supermodel, 1990

'The youth magazines that hot-housed heroin-chic
represented the negotiation of new compromises
in morality, where ideas of deviance become fluid
as new identities are continually experimented
with, pushing at boundaries of acceptability
in representation and attempting to create an
aesthetic that is truer to young people's experiences.'

Rebecca Arnold, fashion historian and critic, 2001

N — NAILS

Coloured nails can be dated back to Ancient China and Egypt when women used products derived from natural sources, such as henna. In Egypt, royalty wore the deepest shades of red, the upper echelons of society were permitted a lighter shade, whilst those at the bottom of the social hierarchy were allowed only the palest shades of pink. Modern nail varnish was introduced in the 1920s and was popularized by Hollywood's film stars.

NAILS

'A well-shaped nail should show something of the delicate pink which we see in sea-shells.'

Modern Etiquette in Private and Public, 1891

'Fingertips and Toetips

No bizarre tones of gold, silver, green or blue. Use pink, coral or red shades. (Exceptions to this rule are the use of iridescents, gold and silver for evening).'

Helena Rubenstein, Beauty scientist and entrepreneur, 1964

NAMES

'Name dropping never improves a conversation.'

Vogue's Book of Etiquette and Good Manners, 1969

NATIONAL ASSETS

'Bureaucrats may smile, but the look of our women is important to our trade as a nation.'

Betty Page, fashion industry and etiquette writer, 1954

NATURE

'Nature has not made us all in the same mould, and we must be careful not to affront Nature, but must accept her gifts and make the best of them.'

Nora M. Bickley, etiquette writer, 1956

'A woman's natural quality is to attract, and having attracted, to enchain; and how influential she may be for good or evil, the history of every age makes clear.'

Mrs H.R. Haweis, writer on fashion and interiors, 1878

NEATNESS

'The eyes of those who form our home circle should never be distressed by an untidy appearance. Circumstances may forbid our garments being either rich or costly, but neatness and simple elegance can always be shown in every dress and at every season.'

Manners of Modern Society, 1877

NEVER

'Ladies are never expected to invade the privacy of the smoking room, and those ladies who are masculine enough to do so often offend against good taste, and their presence, if tolerated, is as unusual as it is undesired.'

Manners and Rules of Good Society or Solecisms to be Avoided, 1893

'Never combine two different materials in the same class; that is, never two different furs, laces, crêpes, wools, cottons, or tweeds.'

Margaretta Byers, fashion writer, 1938

'Never boast of your wealth, your money, your grand friends, or anything that is yours.'

Nora M. Bickley, etiquette writer, 1956

NEW LOOK

Some condemned it as anachronistic and a profligate waste of fabric in a time of acute shortages, but the New Look was so successful that it accounted for 75% of fashion exports from France in 1947.

This was the phrase coined by Carmel Snow, editor of *Harper's Bazaar*, to describe Christian Dior's first collection, shown February 12 1947, officially called the 'Corolle': it has been called the New Look ever since.

'In December 1946, as a result of the war and uniforms, women still looked and dressed like Amazons. But I designed clothes for flower-like women, with rounded shoulders, full feminine busts, and hand span waists above enormous spreading skirts.'

Christian Dior, Parisian fashion designer, 1957

NYLON

'Choose materials which will cooperate with you and crease as little as possible. This does not mean an all-nylon wardrobe – far from it. Avoid transparent nylon dresses as you would the devil.'

Madge Garland, editor of Vogue and founding Professor of the Royal College of Art's fashion department, 1958

O — OPERA CLOAK

An evening cloak, usually full-length, made from an ornate or lavishly worked fabric, which was popular from around 1900 to 1939.

ON THE VALUE OF OBSERVATION

'Everyone probably knows that silly story of the man and the woman passing down the street and meeting another woman. When they had gone by, the man with the woman said, "Did you notice that person?" and his companion replied "You mean the woman with the halo hat in grey with iridescent feathers, a navy suit with a gardenia on the lapel, twisted pearl choker, black gloves, nylon pumps and a slightly turned-over heel on the right shoe?" To which he replies "Yes", and she answers "No, not particularly. Why?"'

Betty Page, fashion industry and etiquette writer, 1954

OPERA

At the opera:

'Full evening dress and beautiful jewels are *de rigueur*.'

Mrs Eric Pritchard, journalist and writer, 1902

OVERDRESSED

'A woman can never be overdressed in my clothes; nothing is worse than being overdressed, and that goes for the mind too. A woman showing off intellectually is as bad as a woman wearing satin for breakfast.'

Gabrielle 'Coco' Chanel, Parisian fashion designer, 1954

P — PERFUME

A substance, usually liquid, with an appealing fragrance. Many fashion designers have their own perfume: Parisian couturier Paul Poiret was the first to do this and Chanel was the first designer to use her name when she launched Chanel No. 5 in 1921.

PARIS

(see also Haute Couture, page 57)

'Whenever the word fashion is mentioned, almost instantly Paris comes to mind as its associate term. It is almost as if Paris and fashion were synonymous.'

Paul Nystrom, Director of America's Retail Research Association 1921–7, 1928

'The Parisienne, it's a navy blue blazer, a black turtleneck and a black suede skirt. Red nails. It's a very simple image yet very significant. It's very carefully thought accessories.'

Yves Saint Laurent, Parisian fashion designer, 1936–2008

'In Paris, fashion is not frivolity; it is the most important of all the decorative arts. And Collection time is the culmination of six months of creative thinking, supported by intense business activities within every section of France's second largest industry ... it is not only in the couture houses themselves that the tense 'First Night' atmosphere prevails. The lighting upon the chandeliers in the salons marks the commencement of a dream in which innumerable ancillary trades have a stake:

fabric manufacturers, shoemakers, milliners, furriers, leather merchants, makers of buttons, belts, buckles, handbags, umbrellas; purveyors of ribbons and laces and sophisticated faces; hairdressers, embroiderers, jewellers. Representatives of all these trades are in Paris; and amongst them various strange, extraneous species.'

Alison Adburgham, Vogue editor, journalist and fashion historian, 1960

PERFUME

Paris, 1930s:

'To find the name of a perfume is a very difficult problem because every word in the dictionary seems to be registered. The colour flashed in front of my eyes. Bright, impossible, impudent, becoming, life-giving, like all the light and birds and the fish in the world put together, a colour of China and Peru but not of the West – a shocking colour, pure and undiluted. So I called the perfume "Shocking."'

Elsa Schiaparelli, Parisian fashion designer, 1954

'A perfume is an open door on a rediscovered universe.'

Christian Dior, Parisian fashion designer, 1905–57

POCKET

Edward III 1327–77

'Pocket. A pouch or bag. They first appear in the illuminations of the time of Edward III.'

S. William Beck, writer for the Drapers Journal, 1886

'Pocket: a necessity in every dress, usually useful, but sometimes a line to mark a hip bone – also a place to put your hands.'

Claire McCardell, New York fashion designer, 1956

'Pockets are very important. Take two women, the two dressed with a jersey tube ... the one with pockets will immediately have a feeling of superiority on the other. To let one's arms hang or to feel obliged to cross them or fiddle a ring, are awkward gestures, handicaps.'

Yves Saint Laurent, Parisian fashion designer, 1936–2008

PREMIERE
Head of a department within a couture house.

Q — QUEEN

A female sovereign, a hereditary ruler or wife of a King. The term is also used to describe pre-eminence and has been appropriated by the gay community to describe homosexual men.

'Always on exhibition, but with less freedom than film stars, royal personages are obliged to adhere to rather impersonal rules of elegance.'
Genevieve Antoine Dariaux, Directrice at Nina Ricci (Paris), 1964

'The war brought a new dress problem to the Queen. What should she wear when visiting bombed sites and the devastated areas all over the country? The Queen made a wise decision in adhering to gentle colours.'
Norman Hartnell, London fashion designer and royal dressmaker, 1955

On designing the embroidery motifs for the Queen's coronation dress, Hartnell asked the Garter King of Arms for a daffodil for Wales. He was told the correct emblem was a leek:

'The leek I agreed was a most admirable vegetable, full of historic significance and doubtless of health-giving properties, but scarcely noted for its beauty … in the end, by using lovely silks and sprinkling it with the dew diamonds, we were able to transform the earthy leek into a vision of Cinderella charm and worthy of mingling with her sisters Rose and Mimosa in a brilliant Royal Assembly, and fit to embellish the dress of a queen.'
Norman Hartnell, London fashion designer and royal dressmaker, 1955

'Whereas clothes for royal ladies are always made in colours which are distinctive enough not to merge into the background against which they will be seen, hats, on the contrary, must not obtrude too obviously.'
Aage Thaarup, London milliner, 1956

R — RIBBONS AND RUFFLES

Narrow strip of fabric, often with a corded finish at both edges, used primarily to decorate or trim. Also used as regalia and insignia to identify membership.

READY-TO-WEAR

The sewing machine was introduced in 1846 and helped facilitate the mass production of clothing. However, it was not until the 1920s that women's fashionable clothing became widely available ready-made, when high fashion no longer required a figure-moulding fit, and rayon, which superficially resembled the look and feel of natural silk but cost a third of the price, became available. In France, ready-to-wear is called prêt-a-porter.

REGRET

'As it is ill-mannered to express too much regret, so it is the essence of rudeness not to make any apology.'

Manners of Modern Society, 1877

'I do regret the passing of so much of the romance which made the world a very pleasant place in the past. It is possible to look upon realities too much, so that you lose the power of make-believe, and I think that perhaps is a mistake which we are all making today.'

Lady Duff Gordon, the London fashion designer Lucile, 1932

RIBBONS FOR DECORATION AND ORNAMENT

In the 1930s, Anglo-American couturier Charles James made various versions of his ribbon ball dress and cape, created using pre-war grosgrain millinery ribbons from Colcombet of Saint-Étienne, who wove the finest quality ribbons. By the 1950s, he was based in New York: Balenciaga described him as the greatest American couturier. Mrs Hearst was wearing Charles James:

'Varieties of ribbons – Every personality and mood can be satisfied, for there are severe-looking ribbons, fluffy, frivolous ribbons and all kinds between these extremes. A visit to the ribbon counter of any large department store will disclose grosgrain ribbons for tailored costume, lovely moiré, taffeta and satin ribbons, plain, figured and plaid ribbons and dainty picot and metal-edged ribbons so charming on the young girl's party frocks.'

Dress Decoration and Ornament, 1925

'Named to the "Best Dressed" list in 1956 – as well as in several other years – Mrs Hearst is seen in a gown of tulle and satin that is quite literally "staggering": not only is it a marvel of construction but the wearer can barely move in it.'

Elizabeth Ann Coleman, fashion historian and curator, 1986

RIDING

'A lady's hunting dress is plain and useful, but a very becoming one withal. It consists of a dark-coloured tight-fitting habit, made with not very long skirt, or it will get sadly bespattered with mud. A plain linen collar is worn round the throat, fastened by a bow of bright ribbon. Linen cuffs and white leather gloves finish the costume.'

Manners of Modern Society, 1877

'A woman can scarcely be expected to have the agility to mount her horse from the ground without assistance, though, with a well-trained horse, she may readily mount from the steps of a horse-block. But the best horse-block is a friend that knows his duty, and a sensible woman will have no other.'

Complete Etiquette for Ladies and Gentlemen, 1900

'Hacking is leisurely country riding. Blue jeans and a shirt or sweater are the most informal clothes one can wear, but they are not precisely traditional.'

Vogue's Book of Etiquette and Good Manners, 1969

RUFFLES

A jabot is a frill or ruffle worn down the front of a bodice (which clothes the upper body), and is derived from 18th century menswear.

'I like the idea that a ruffle seems to come from nothing. I like things that are sculptural and yet are soft.'

Halston, New York fashion designer, 1932–90

S — SHOES

A pair of protective foot coverings that reach no higher than the ankle (when the term boot is used).

SCARVES

'A scarf is to a woman what a necktie is to a man, and the way you tie it is part of your personality.'

Christian Dior, Parisian fashion designer, 1954

THE SEASON

'Everything revolved around the courts in summer, the presentation of débutante daughters, nieces and cousins; with at least one big dance between May and July, at the end of which the houses were theoretically empty, the owners being on their way north to the moors, via Goodwood and Ascot.'

Norman Hartnell, London fashion designer and royal dressmaker, 1955

SEQUINS

Sequins were made in Italy from the 13th century.

'The ugly can be elegant; the vulgar never. And vulgarity nearly always begins with sequins. When sequins fall into the wrong hands, all appears to be lost and there is no saying what may happen.'

Alison Adburgham, retail historian and journalist, 1957

SHOES

'In selecting shoes to wear with certain dresses, exercise great care to have the leather of the shoes correspond with the texture of the dress. For instance, soft silk dresses, such as charmeuse and satin, are really better with low fine kid or patent leather shoes and, the shoes being low, silk stockings help to soften the lines of the foot.'

Mary Brooks-Picken, writer on making, interpreting and designing fashion, 1918

Ferragamo incorporated materials such as lace and raffia into his finely crafted shoes and was known for his signature prow (upturned) toe and wedge cork soled shoes. He designed flat-heeled shoes for Greta Garbo and stiletto heels for Marilyn Monroe.

'Women must be persuaded that luxury shoes need not be painful to walk in; they must be convinced that it is possible to wear the most refined and exotic footwear because we now know how to design a supportive shoe.'

Salvatore Ferragamo, Florentine shoe designer, 1956 .

'Should you see a shoe which allures you as a thing of beauty in itself, buy it by all means, if it is becoming, but wear it, please, with the simplest of dresses.'

Ernestine Carter, fashion writer and The Sunday Times editor, 1958

'The secret of toe cleavage, a very important part of the sexuality of the shoe, is you must only show the first two cracks.'

Manolo Blahnik, London shoemaker, 2008

'Thanks in part to Sex And The City, Manolo Blahnik has become one of the handful of designers whose name is synonymous with their product. In his case, it is his Christian name, because "Manolo" is now used as slang to describe very expensive, very beautiful shoes: even by the millions of people who have never actually seen a pair of Manolo Blahniks and could not dream of spending $300 or $400 to buy them.'

Design Museum London, 2008

'I selected the colour red because it is engaging, flirtatious, memorable and the colour of passion.'
Christian Louboutin, Parisian shoemaker, 2007

'The flash of scarlet sends out a subliminal messages to shoe princesses everywhere.'
Suzy Menkes, fashion writer and International Herald Tribune editor, 2005

SHOPPING

'Buy with judgement and wear with intention.'
Mrs Eric Pritchard, journalist and writer, 1902

'For some temperaments, the relish lies in acts of acquisition, for others in risking a series of delicious temptations, for others again in demonstration of their own judgement and common sense.'
Doris Langley-Moore, fashion collector, curator and historian, 1953

'The woman who gives in to impulsive, thoughtless buying can waste more pounds in a short time than many well-dressed women spend in several years, and all the money in the world can't prevent an uncontrolled woman from looking a mess.'
Betty Page, fashion industry and etiquette writer, 1954

'It is seldom possible to recognize a bargain at the time you buy it, because the true cost of a garment is not necessarily the sum that is marked on the price tag. In order to find out how much it really cost you, you would have to take this price and divide it by the number of times you wear the article in question, and then accord generous bonus points for the pleasure, self-confidence and elegance it may have given you.'

Genevieve Antoine Dariaux, Directrice at Nina Ricci (Paris), 1964

SHOULDERS

'I have often amused myself by thinking of the shapes of women's shoulders in terms of bottles: hock bottles in 1840, claret bottles in 1890, and in 1946 – well! Gin bottles!'

James Laver, V&A curator and historian of fashion imagery, 1946

SMART

'The aggressiveness of the Smart Woman
To pick holes in the smart woman is impossible, for she won't allow it. She has come as a wave from a new world; and what is more, she has come to stay.'

Mrs Eric Pritchard, journalist and writer, 1902

SPACE AGE FASHION

Paris, 1965:

'The Courrèges collection is shown at a fierce pace, to *musique concrête*, with taut precision. At this house, tape measures are surely replaced by slide rules. Aggressive clothes are cut with fiendish genius. Seams are so architecturally part of the structure that they appear welded rather than sewn. Dresses are four inches above the knee; for evening they are the same length, made of serried sequins. Underclothes are a matter of conjecture – most probably one-piece nude leotards, adhesive for fit.'

Alison Adburgham, Vogue editor, journalist and fashion historian, 1965

SPORTSWEAR

The rise of physical activity for women in the mid 1860s led to especially designed sportswear such as tailor-made walking costumes, croquet dress and swimwear:

'The freewheel has revolutionized the whole idea of dress ... it is quite permissible to cycle in the smartest Louis XV shoes; thus your foot can look as pretty on a bicycle as with your best toilette, though alas! the cycling woman seldom avails herself of this privilege. Why in the name of all that is beautiful should the seekers after health make themselves as hideous and ungraceful as possible?'

Mrs Eric Pritchard, journalist and writer, 1902

The 1930s was the era when health and fitness came to the fore. Claire McCardell introduced sturdy denim fabrics to designer fashion – snug wool dresses with hoods and the type of leotards and shoes worn by dancers:

'The beach costume is sometimes of velvet, with cap and capes to match, or one piece taffeta, or of silk jersey with a short peplum and shirred knickers, or of gingham or printed silk.'

Margaret Story, fashion and etiquette writer, 1924

'I'd always wondered why women's clothes had to be delicate – why couldn't they be practical and sturdy as well as feminine?'

Claire McCardell, New York fashion designer, 1948

'Typists cycle to the country at weekends in shorts no more ample than a loincloth and arouse no comment. And the youth of England eagerly copy American styles of beachwear in the shape of sarongs or shirts made in flowered material, like the loose covers of country house armchairs.'

Pearl (Polly) Binder, graphic artist and dress historian 1953

'Alligator is strictly for sports or travel, shoes as well as bags, and this respected reptile should be permitted to retire every evening at 5pm.'

Genevieve Antoine Dariaux, Directrice at Nina Ricci (Paris), 1964

On his topless monokini: 'By 1964, I'd gone so far with swimwear cut outs that I decided the body itself – including breasts – could become an integral part of a suit's design ... I had no intention of producing the suit for actual consumption until I talked to Diana Vreeland of *Vogue*.'

Rudi Gernreich, New York fashion designer, 1991

STYLE AND STYLISHNESS

STYLE 'the distinctive manner of a person or school.'

STYLISH 'fashionable; elegant. Having a superior quality and manner.'

Oxford English Dictionary, 1991

'Divorce yourself from styles that do not suit you, even though your soul yearns for them.'

Edith Head, Hollywood costume designer, 1959

'Like an artist finds his style, a woman must find hers. And when she is conscious of it, whatever the fashion of the moment is, she is sure to possess a power of seduction.'

Yves Saint Laurent, Parisian fashion designer, 1936–2008

'Try to find out what style is by considering what it is not… style is not wearing curlers and unattractive garments among family members so that one can be a ravishing beauty for strangers.'

Grace Margaret Morton, fashion professor and writer, 1964

'Style is a reflection of personal choice and fashion today is a reflection of personal style.'

Terry Jones, editor of i-D magazine, 2002

SUNGLASSES

'Sunglasses were the first spectacles to become accessories to the feminine mode. This was when it became the thing to go to the French Riviera in the dazzling summer instead of, as before, only in the sunshine of the winter months. Dark glasses, through this association, came to give an air of continental chic and idle richness.'

Alison Adburgham, Vogue editor, journalist and fashion historian, 1955

T — TROUSERS

A garment which encloses the legs and extends from the waist to below the knee. First worn by women in the nineteenth century as riding dress, worn beneath a voluminous skirt and referred to as a 'bifurcated garment'.

TAILORING

'There is a tailor-made type of girl who invariably wears a strong boot, whether she be walking on London pavements or ploughed fields. She is very aggressive, is that tailor-made girl, especially about the feet.'

Mrs Eric Pritchard, journalist and writer, 1902

In autumn/winter 1966, Yves Saint Laurent introduced 'le smoking' - tailored suits with skirts or trousers for women based on black, satin trimmed men's formal eveningwear:

'The cult of the tailor-made is understood now in London just as well as it is in Paris and New York, and many of our leading firms make a speciality of quite inexpensive French tailor-made garments.'

The Ladies Realm, 1906

'I only like sparse luxury. A girl in a black tuxedo.'

Yves Saint Laurent, Parisian fashion designer, 1936–2008

TARTAN

'No fabric means quite as much to both traditionalists and rebels alike.'

Luella Bartley, British fashion designer and writer, 2010

TASTE

'But why do you worry about good taste? That's part of the problem – the worry, the eternal worry. Lots of people have terrible taste, you know, and make a damn good living off of it.'

Diana Vreeland, curator and editor of Harpers Bazaar and American Vogue, 1980

'Taste cannot be taught, but can be acquired. You must be born with the good taste of wishing to acquire good taste.'

Hardy Amies, London fashion designer and royal dressmaker, 1954

THRIFT

'A woman who can only afford to buy one dress generally goes to such trouble to choose it that she makes a good buy. She very often achieves more elegance than the woman who possesses several.'

Christian Dior, Parisian fashion designer, 1957

TIARA

A crown like ornament, or headdress, often set with stones, which is worn by women with formal dress or at their wedding.

'The tiara, the most elegant and dramatic of all jewels, has the unique ability to make a bride feel and look the centre of attention. It is the endorsement of her status as queen of the day.'

Geoffrey Munn, jewellery historian, 2002

TOPLESS

(see Sportswear, page 107)

'A line introduced by American designer Rudi Geinreich, which was immediately given all kinds of cartoonist and/or scurrilous publicity. In other words, the time was not right, but I am sure that it will once again be acceptable for young girls and women of the Western world to expose their breasts as they have done before and as they do in other continents. The present trend towards see-through dresses and no-bras indicates that it is only one step away.'

Janey Ironside, Professor of Fashion Design, Royal College of Art, 1968

TROUSERS

In October 1898, Lady Harberton went to the Hautboy Hotel in Surrey, England, for refreshments after a cycle ride. She was refused entry because she was wearing what was described, at the time, as Rational Dress, which comprised of full, tailored bloomers that reached to just below the knee. The Cyclist's Touring Club, of which she was a member, took the hotel to court, but lost the case.

'We consider this article of dress unnecessary, and in many ways detrimental to health and morals.'

The Lancet, 1879

'Trousers worn for riding are, for the time being, almost out of fashion. There are however, a certain number of ladies who take a more limited amount of horse exercise, and ladies of more advanced age who prefer trousers.'

T.H. Holding, writer on tailoring, 1901

'Legs have emerged after centuries of shrouding, and adult woman at last frankly admits herself to be a biped.'

J.C. Flugel, social psychologist, 1930

England, 1918:

'I had just got clothes like the women-on-the-land were wearing, and in the unaccustomed freedom of breeches and gaiters, I went into wild spirits; I ran, I shouted, I jumped, I climbed, I vaulted over gates, I felt like a schoolboy let out on a holiday.'

Vita Sackville-West, author, poet and gardener, 1973

'If trousers are abominable for women, they are abominable for men.'

Eric Gill, sculptor, typographer and draughtsman, 1931

Wartime Siren Suit from 1939-45:

'The principle effect so far that the war has had on feminine fashions is the production of the "Siren Suit", a sort of masculine overall, often with a hood, and zip fastening, which can be assumed in a moment when the air raid sirens give their warning. They say a good deal of attention is given to the cut so that it may give the wearer an attractive appearance, so necessary of course when she is about to be blown into fragments, in which case her charm will abruptly cease.'

C.Willett Cunnington, fashion collector and historian, 1948

'Trousers should never replace a skirt for everyday wear; and it is on the while a safe and sound principle to treat slacks on the same footing as a housecoat – as something pleasant and easy to wear in your leisure hours at home.'

Ira Morris, designer and art editor, 1947

'The variety of fabrics that are used in lounging pyjamas, the informal garments that are worn during hours of relaxation at home, is very wide indeed. For sleeping purposes, however, the fabrics most popularly used are washable – cotton challis, poplin, percale, chambray, shantung, broadcloth, sateen, Madras, plisse crêpe, flannelette, outing flannel – or crêpe and satin made of nylon, acetate, rayon or silk, in the luxury type of garment.'

Mary Evans, fashion and etiquette writer, 1952

'Shorts, jeans, trousers resembling ballet tights (due to the French influence which always succeeds in tightening even the most masculine styles so as to display the feminine figure more closely), are all popular women's wear for beach or "play."'

Pearl (Polly) Binder, graphic artist & dress historian, 1953

In the early 1960s, Parisian couturier André Courrèges introduced Space Age white and silver trouser suits for women. The vogue for unisex clothes was the first time trouser suits for women became widely fashionable.

'A woman is seductive wearing trousers only if she wears them with all her femininity. Not like a George Sand. Trousers are a coquetry, an added charm, not a sign of equality or emancipation.'

Yves Saint Laurent, Parisian fashion designer, 1936–2008

Bumsters – the name given to Alexander McQueen's low-rise trousers from 1996.

TROUSSEAU

The clothes that a bride takes on her honeymoon and in preparation for her new life as a married woman.

U — UMBRELLA

Introduced in Europe in the seventeenth century, initially as a sunshade for women (suntans were avoided at all costs and were considered the burden of working women until the 1920s). The collapsible ribs were made of whalebone or cane, covered by oiled silk or linen. By 1800, the pagoda shape was common and in 1835 the tubular metal frame was patented.

> 'It is a good idea to have one umbrella and many covers for it – then you can have a colour that goes with every outfit.'
>
> *Christian Dior, Parisian fashion designer, 1954*

UNISEX

His 'n' Her boutique opened in Carnaby Street, London, 1965, by John Stephen.

V — VANITY CASE

A container to carry cosmetics and toiletries.

> 'Even the vanity case has been made so alluring that it is impossible to frown at the insouciant user.'
>
> *Margaret Story, fashion and etiquette writer, 1924*

VEILS

> 'Veil: literally that which bears a ship onward; a sail, a covering, a curtain, anything that hides an object; a piece of muslin or thin cloth worn by ladies to the face; a disguise.'
>
> *The Drapers Dictionary*

> 'This accessory is a very important one, and fashion has often much to answer for in the freaks and fancies indulged in by the designers and manufacturers.'
>
> *Mrs Eric Pritchard, journalist and writer, 1902*

> 'Veils, like perfume, are an exquisite luxury if they are dainty, delicate and becoming.'
>
> *Mary Brooks-Picken, writer on making, interpreting and designing fashion, 1918*

VENDEUSE

Each couture client has her own vendeuse who assists her selection of models – she must build her trust, as it is well known that the vendeuse works on commission:

'Successful sales are like icebergs – one-eighth visible above water. The other seven-eighths consist of the relationship between vendeuse and client. I find at the moment when a sale is about to be clinched, a tenuous relationship grows up between the two people concerned. If someone breaks the thread, we may lose the sale.'

Ginnette Spanier, Directrice of the House of Balmain, 1959

VINTAGE AND DIY STYLE

A term used to refer to fashions from a previous era, sometimes as recently as 15 years ago, that are juxtaposed and worn with new clothes to create a distinctive style.

'The scarf may have belonged to our grandmother, the flower may be taken out of an old hat, the jewel a false one bought from a stall in a street market: if the effect is good, our sense of achievement is all the greater for that.'

Doris Langley-Moore, fashion collector, curator and historian, 1953

'DIY! Don't buy my clothes. Well, if you are rich or can afford a stylist, you can get me. But if not, do it yourself. My idea is that you can mix charity, vintage, Portobello Road, pieces of Ikat fabric; wrap it all around yourself, use a handkerchief as knickers, mix safety pins and jewellery. But above all do something! Be optimistic!'

Vivienne Westwood, London fashion designer, 2008

ON FASHION CYCLES
The same costume will be...

Indecent	10 years before its time	
Shameless	5 " "	
Outré (daring)	1 " "	
Smart	_____	
Dowdy	1 year after its time	
Hideous	10 " "	
Ridiculous	20 " "	
Amusing	30 " "	
Quaint	50 " "	
Charming	70 " "	
Romantic	100 " "	
Beautiful	150 " "	

James Laver, V&A curator and historian of fashion imagery, 1937

W — WEDDING DRESS

A ceremonial garment, often with a train and worn with a veil, introduced in the nineteenth century (before this, there was not a prescribed formula, although women usually wore a white dress).

WEARABILITY

'It's funny how certain words go in and out of vogue. In the sixties, the dirtiest word in fashion was wearable. Nobody wanted to be known for wearable clothes, although I was.'

Bill Blass, New York fashion designer, 2002

WEDDINGS AND MARRIAGE

'The origin of the custom of wearing the wedding ring upon the fourth finger of the left hand has been much disputed. The most reasonable inference, however, as to its origin, appears to be its convenience.'

Daisy Eyebright, etiquette writer and contributor to the 'Woman's Page' of Country Gentleman, 1884

'The veil, as we use it, may be a substitute for the flowing tresses which in old times, fell like a mantle modestly concealing the bride's face and form.'

Emily Post, etiquette writer, 1875

'Whatever her preconceived notions of independence may be, a girl has, when she is first married, a spontaneous eagerness for looking after her man in her own home. There is then, for a while, a magic and glamour about domesticity. It is only later that she remembers she is a free woman with a grudge against domestic entanglements.'

Margaret Kornitzer, writer on family life, adoption and women, 1929

'A bride who is a widow should not wear white, nor a bridal veil, nor a wreath of orange blossoms nor orange blossom on her dress. She should not be attended by bridesmaids, and wedding favours should not be worn by the guests.'

Manners and Rules of Good Society or Solecisms to be Avoided, 1902

WHAT TO WEAR
'WHAT TO WEAR TO YOUR OWN PARTY

If you give a tea, you are supposed to dress more formally than your guests. The theory is that they will come in street clothes, probably suits or tailored dresses. While you, being at home, should be discovered in an afternoon frock.

WHAT TO WEAR TO SOMEONE ELSE'S PARTY

Sometimes your hostess gives you clues by saying "black tie" or "white tie". Black tie means semi-formality; dinner dresses with covered décolletages or dinner suits. When she says "white tie", you go to the limit of formality. When she gives you no clues, underdress rather than overdress. You will always be more comfortable.'

Margaretta Byers, fashion writer, 1939

WHITE SHIRT

'My favourite piece of clothing is the white shirt. In general, fashion designers say, "I wish I had invented jeans". I would have loved to invent the white shirt.'

Karl Lagerfeld, Parisian designer and photographer, 2011

'WHY DON'T YOU?'

The name of Diana Vreeland's witty column in American *Harpers Bazaar*, published from 1936. Such as, 'Why Don't You ... turn your old ermine coat into a bathrobe?'

WIGS

'Our coloured wigs became an important accessory. My aunt had told me how when she went on long journeys to India, she would have a little row of false curls to use when her hair was not in the right condition. She would put on a close fitting cap, stuff the curls round the edge, and presto – she would look her immaculate self again. I had similar curls made on a piece of wire but, for Biba, they were dipped into lots of unnatural colours – navies, violets, mulberry and bright henna. They proved very useful on photographic sessions to cut down on hairdressing time.'

Barbara Hulanicki, London fashion designer, 1983

X, Y, Z — ZIP

Abbreviation of zipper, a copyrighted trade name for a slide fastener. This mechanism was patented in 1903 but zips were not widely available until the 1930s. Elsa Schiaparelli and Charles James endorsed 'lightning' zips from the mid-1930s and made a feature of the mechanism: traditionally fastenings were concealed. In the 1970s, they became part of the stylistic iconography of sub-cultural punks.

X-RAY DRESS

Paris, 1927:

'There was a skeleton sweater that shocked the bourgeois but hit the newspapers, which then took little note of fashion. White lines on the sweaters followed the design of the ribs so that women wearing it gave the appearance of being seen through an X-ray.'

Elsa Schiaparelli, Parisian fashion designer, 1954

'Garments of striking transparency were worn in 1912 and known as X-ray dresses.'

Paul Nystrom, writer on the fashion industry, 1928

YACHTING DRESS

'Yachting dresses are generally made of serge or weed, as being unspoilable by sea, air and water, and at the same time possessing warmth and durability.'

Manners of Modern Society, 1877

YARN

'Term applied to the product of any spinning mill whether the basic fibre be wool, cotton, linen, silk, rayon, or other fibre. Tarns are used for weaving, knitting, and crocheting. They are continuous threads of spun fibres – animal, mineral, vegetable or man-made.'

Mary Brooks-Picken, writer on making, interpreting and designing fashion, 1918

YOUTH

'Youth has been granted privileges that it never had before, and maturity has willingly forgone its former dignities in return for the right of sharing in the appearance and activities of youth.'

J.C. Flugel, social psychologist, 1930

'Seventeen: Not Too Sweet

Innocent airs and cute tricks

Run black or bright ribbon through an off-the-shoulder neckline. Wear a posy at the waist of a plain dark dress. Wear a jewel or a flower on a crossed velvet ribbon at your throat with a low-necked dress.

Romance and rhythm

Always have a swing skirt for dancing. Show off pretty ears by tying your hair back with a black Mozart bow. Have a frou frou petticoat to swish beneath your dance frock. Have a hooded shoulder-cape of lace to top a picture-dress. Wear flowers on a ribbon at your wrist for a dinner-date.'

Ira Morris, designer and art editor, 1947

'One day, I pulled on an eight-year-old boy's sweater for fun. I was enchanted with the result. And, in six months, all the birds were wearing the skinny-ribs that resulted.'

Mary Quant, London fashion designer, 1965

ZEST

'Anything you do, work or pleasure, you have to do it with zest. You have to live with zest ... and that is the secret of beauty and fashion, too. There is no beauty that is attractive without zest. There is no fashion which is good without care, enthusiasm and zest behind it. Zest in designing ... zest in making ... and zest in wearing your clothes.'

Christian Dior, Parisian fashion designer, 1954

ZIPS

On Charles James:

'The employment of the new was always a challenge to James; in 1933, he took the zipper and spun it round the torso by inserting it into his "Taxi" dress ... packaged in sealed cellophane envelopes, it was made in two sizes, an early attempt by James to demonstrate that detailed sizing was not essential if a garment was designed correctly.'

Elizabeth Ann Coleman, fashion historian and curator, 1986

'Zip. Colloquial term for life, dash, sparkle. To move quickly; to close with a slide-fastener.'

Mary Brooks-Picken, writer on making, interpreting and designing fashion, 1918

Details on Illustrations

Page 3 Silk and tulle shoes by Roger Vivier for Christian Dior, Paris, 1954, V&A: T.148–1974.

Page 6 Fan, produced for Omega studios, painted by Duncan Grant, Britain, 1913, V&A: CIRC. 260–1964.

Page 8 'Super-elevated Ghillie' platform shoes by Vivienne Westwood, Britain, 1993, V&A: T.225:1, 2–1993.

Page 25 Leather shoes with stencilled decoration, Britain, c.1800, V&A: T.115&A–1933.

Page 37 Design drawing by The Roseland Studio, made for Willetts & Sons, Britain, 1920s, V&A: E.3219–2004.

Page 40 *Top:* Fan, produced for Omega studios, painted by Duncan Grant, Britain, 1913, V&A: CIRC. 260–1964.

Bottom: Fan, produced by Eventails Gane for Dior, France, 1950–55, V&A: T.31–1983.

Page 43 Pink straw cloche hat with appliqué trim made by Kilpin Ltd, Britain, c.1925, V&A: T.442–1977.

Page 53 Kidskin gloves, Britain, 1615–25, V&A: 202&A–1900.

Page 54 *Clockwise from top left:* Embroidered bag by Hilde Wagner-Ascher, Austrian, c.1925, V&A: T.284–1987 / Crocodile-effect leather handbag by Philip Treacy, Britain, 1998, V&A: T.8–1999 / Plastic bag by Elgee, Britain, 1950s, V&A: T.235&A–1982 / Crocodile-effect leather handbag, France, c.1900, V&A: T.203&A–1975 / Black vintage bag not in the collection of the V&A / Velvet and moulded papier-mâché reticule, Britain, 1820–40, V&A: T.449–1985.

Page 64 Platinum and diamond earrings by Cartier, London, 1930–35, V&A: M.206: 1, 2–2007.

Page 66 Necklace, Europe, bow c.1660, chain and pendant 19th century, V&A: M.95–1909.

Page 80 *Clockwise from top left:* Hat with gloves by Eileen Agar and Elsa Schiaparelli, Paris, 1936, V&A: T.169–1993 / White feathered hat not in the collection of the V&A / Hand-stitched goose feather hat by Philip Treacy, Britain, 1995, V&A: T.182–1996 / Hat for eating bouillabaisse by Eileen Agar, Britain, 1937, V&A: T.168–1993 / Tatlin hat by Stephen Jones, Britain, 1982, V&A: T.222–1989 / Hat by Cristóbal

Balenciaga for Eisa, Spain, 1962, V&A: T.146–1998 / Net and straw hat trimmed with feathers and horsehair, Britain, 1938–40, V&A: T.36–1986 / Hat with black ribbon not in the collection of the V&A.

Page 90 Evening cloak by Lucile Ltd, London, c.1915, V&A: T.298–1974.

Page 96 Manchester tiara by Cartier, Paris, 1903, V&A: M.6:1–2007.

Page 102 *Clockwise from top left:* Silk satin shoes by Dior, Paris, c.1960, V&A: T.153&A–1974 (Polka dot lining added by illustrator) / Silk and tulle shoes by Roger Vivier for Dior, Paris, 1954, V&A: T.148–1974 / Leather with punched work shoes by Hook, Knowles & Co., London, c.1900, V&A: T.246A&:1–1979 / Satin shoes, England, 1820–50, V&A: T.547&A–1913 / Silk and kid shoes, Britain, 1780–1800, V&A: T.24&A–1956; Silk boots, Britain or France, 1865–75, V&A: T.180&A–1984 / Leather shoes, Britain, c.1800, V&A: T.115&A–1933.

Page 109 Plastic sunglasses by Oliver Goldsmith Eyewear, Britain, 1967, V&A: T.244U–1990.

Page 113 Trousers by Courrèges, France, 1960s.

Page 143 Straw hat by Aage Thaarup, London, 1960s, V&A: T.261–1985.

Endpapers, *Top row from left:* Net and straw hat trimmed with feathers and horsehair, Britain, 1938–40, V&A: T.36–1986 / Tatlin hat by Stephen Jones, Britain, 1982, V&A: T.222–1989 / Pink straw cloche hat with appliqué trim made by Kilpin Ltd, Britain, c.1925, V&A: T.442–1977 / Hand-stitched goose feather hat by Philip Treacy, Britain, 1995, V&A: T.182–1996.

Middle row from left: Hat with gloves by Eileen Agar and Elsa Schiaparelli, Paris, 1936, V&A: T.169–1993 / Black hat not in the collection of the V&A / Hat with black ribbon not in the collection of the V&A / Hat for eating bouillabaisse by Eileen Agar, Britain, 1937, V&A: T.168–1993.

Bottom row from left: Straw hat by Aage Thaarup, London, 1960s, V&A: T.261–1985 / White feathered hat not in the collection of the V&A. Hat by Cristóbal Balenciaga for Eisa Spain, 1962, V&A: T.146–1993 / Hat not in the collection of the V&A.

Acknowledgements

At V&A Publishing, I thank Mark Eastment, Head of Publishing; Clare Faulkner for initiating the project and persisting in the search for 'the right' illustrator; Frances Ambler for careful editing and fastidious organisation of so, so many references and Clare Davis for managing production. The external editor, Sarah Drinkwater, was meticulous – I am most grateful. It has been a joy to work with Emma Farrarons, whose delightful illustrations animate the book so elegantly.

I am immensely grateful to Valerie D. Mendes, former Head of Textiles & Dress at the V&A, for locating the perfect quotes to fill gaps and for letting me roam free in her incredible library. It also gives me pleasure to acknowledge significant contributions made by my former students, graduates from the MA in Fashion Curation at the London College of Fashion: Hayley Dujardin-Edwards, Helen Ritchie, Jenna Rossi-Camus and Gemma Williams.

And I thank Kevin, who, for three decades, has tolerated ever-growing mountains of books, which I always knew would – each and every one – earn their house space one day!

References

Fashion designers are identified by the major city in which they work/ed and/or present their collections, rather than their place of birth.

Alison Adburgham
Vogue editor 1926–35, journalist and fashion historian (1891–1980)
View of Fashion (London, 1966): 18, 46, 49, 63, 71, 77, 79, 83, 94, 103, 106, 109

Hardy Amies
London fashion designer and royal dressmaker, label Hardy Amies (1909–2003)
Just So Far (London, 1954): 12, 13, 58, 67, 79, 112

Rebecca Arnold
Fashion historian and critic
Fashion, Desire and Anxiety (London, 2001): 85

Bettina Ballard
Editor for French and American *Vogue*
In My Fashion (London, 1960): 44

Luella Bartley
British fashion designer and writer
Luella's Guide to English Style (London, 2010): 111
Reproduced by permission of HarperCollins Publishers Ltd © 2010 Luella Bartley

Cecil Beaton
Writer, photographer, illustrator, costume designer (1904–80)
The Glass of Fashion (London, 1954): 43

S. W. Beck
Writer for the *Drapers Journal*
The Drapers Journal (London, 1886): 49, 52, 94

Celia Bertin
Mannequin
Paris á la Mode (London, 1956): 44, 58

Nora M. Bickley
Etiquette writer
A Manual of Etiquette (London, 1956): 61, 88, 89

Pearl (Polly) Binder
Graphic artist and dress historian (1904–90)
Muffs and Morals (London, 1953): 18, 41, 107, 115

Manolo Blahnik
London shoemaker, label Manolo Blahnik (1942–)
Interview with Colin McDowell on Design Museum's website, http://designmuseum.org/design/manolo-blahnik: 104 (both)

Charles Blanc
Art critic (1813–82)
Art in Ornament and Dress (translated from French, London, 1881): 41

Bill Blass
New York fashion designer, label Bill Blass Limited (1922–2002)
Bill Blass: An American Designer, H. O' Hagan et al (New York, 2002): 17, 25
Bare Blass, C. Horyn, ed. (New York, 2002): 123
Copyright © 2002 by the Estate of Bill Blass. Reprinted by permission of HarperCollins Publishers

Mary Brooks-Picken
Writer on making, interpreting & defining fashion (1886–1981)
The Language of Fashion (New York, 1939): 127, 129
The Secrets of Distinctive Dress (Pennsylvania, 1918): 47, 48, 59, 65, 104, 119

Cora Brown Potter
American actress (1859–1936)
Secrets of Beauty and Mysteries of Health (London, 1908): 27

Margaretta Byers
Fashion writer
Designing Women: the art, technique and cost of being beautiful (London, 1939): 16, 24, 24, 33, 55, 61, 89, 124

Ernestine Carter
Fashion writer and associate editor of *The Sunday Times* 1955–72 (1906–83)
The Intelligent Woman's Guide to Good Taste, S. Chitty (London, 1958): 104

Gabrielle 'Coco' Chanel
Parisian fashion designer, label Chanel (1883–1971)
Chanel: Collections and Creations, D. Bott (London, 2007): 32
Coco Chanel, M. Haedrich (London, 1972): 12
The Allure of Chanel, P. Morand (Paris, 1976): 16, 43, 67
American *Vogue*, 1 October 1926: 16
British *Vogue*, November 1916: 70; February 1954: 91

Elizabeth Ann Coleman
Fashion historian and curator
The Genius of Charles James (New York, 1986): 100, 129

Noel Coward
Playwright, composer and director (1889–1973)
Introduction to *It Isn't All Mink*, G. Spanier (London, 1959): 49

C. Willett Cunnington
Fashion collector and historian
The Perfect Lady (London, 1948): 12, 24, 29, 75, 76
Looking Over my Shoulder (London, 1961): 114

Lilly Daché
New York milliner and fashion designer, label Lilly Daché (1898–1989)
Talking Through My Hats (New York, 1956): 83

Genevieve Antoine Dariaux
Directrice at the House of Nina Ricci (Paris)
Elegance (London, 1964): 15, 19, 21, 23, 34, 37, 38, 39, 52, 56, 77, 97, 105, 108
Reproduced by permission of HarperCollins Publishers Ltd © 1964 Genevieve
Antoine Dariaux

Ann Demeulemeester
Belgian fashion designer, label Ann Demeulemeester (1959–)
Fashion Now, T. Jones and S. Rushton (Cologne; London, 2003): 44

Christian Dior
Parisian fashion designer, label Christian Dior (1905–57)
Christian Dior, M. Pochna (Paris, 1994): 16, 35, 94
Christian Dior: The Man Who Made the World Look New, M. Pochna (New York, 1996): 117
Dior by Dior (London, 2007): 44, 103
Little Dictionary of Fashion (London, 2007): 11, 12, 18, 19, 35 (both), 38, 46, 49, 52,
83, 89, 112, 129

Lady Duff Gordon
London fashion designer, label Lucile (1863–1935)
Discretions and Indiscretions (London, 1932): 85, 99

Anne Edwards and Drusilla Dreyfus
Writers on fashion and etiquette
Lady Behave (London, 1956): 48

Perry Ellis
New York fashion designer, label Perry Ellis (1940–86)
Quoted by John Duka, *New York Times Magazine* (New York, 1978): 32

Linda Evangelista
Canadian supermodel (1965–)
Widely quoted in the press: 85

Caroline Evans
Fashion historian and critic
Fashion at the Edge (New Haven, 2003): 45

Mary Evans
Writer on fashion and etiquette
Better Clothes for Your Money (Philadelphia; New York, 1952): 114

Daisy Eyebright
Writer on etiquette and contributor to the 'Woman's Page' of *Country Gentleman*
Manual of Etiquette (London, 1884): 65, 74, 82 (both), 123

Salvatore Ferragamo
Florentine shoe designer, label Ferragamo (1898–1960)
Salvatore Ferragamo (London, 1995): 104

J.C. Flugel
Social psychologist (1884–1955)
The Psychology of Clothes (London, 1930): 19, 27, 55, 113, 128

Anne Fogarty
New York fashion designer (1919–80)
The Art of Being a Well-Dressed Wife (London, 2011): 19, 22, 44, 57, 62, 67, 78

George P. Fox
Writer on the influence of fashion
Fashion: The Power that Influences the World (New York, 1871): 24, 42

Hadley Freeman
Fashion journalist (1978–)
The Meaning of Sunglasses (London, 2009): 56, 73

Akiko Fukai
Curator of Kyoto Costume Institute
Future Beauty: 30 Years of Japanese Fashion, A. Fukai et al (London, 2010): 69

John Galliano
London fashion designer, labels Galliano and John Galliano (1960)
Quoted by Oriole Cullen, *Hats: An Anthology* by Stephen Jones (London, 2009): 84

Madge Garland
Editor of *Vogue* and founding Professor of the Royal College of Art's fashion department (1898–1990)
Fashion (London, 1962): 44
The Intelligent Woman's Guide to Good Taste, S.Chitty (London, 1958): 89

Rudi Gernreich
New York fashion designer, label Rudi Gernreich (1922–85)
The Rudi Gernreich book, P. Moffit and W. Claxton (London, 1991): 108

Eric Gill
Sculptor, typographer, draughtsman (1882–1940)
Clothes (London, 1931): 114

Howard Greer
Lucile's assistant and Hollywood costume designer (1896–1974)
Designing Male (London, 1952): 85

Halston
Full name Roy Halston Frowick, New York fashion designer, label Halston (1932–)
Halston an American Original, E. Gross and F. Rottman (London, 1999): 101

Norman Hartnell
London fashion designer and royal dressmaker, label Norman Hartnell (1901–79)
Silver and Gold (London, 1955): 31, 52, 79, 97 (both), 103

Mrs H.R. Haweis
Writer on fashion and interiors
The Art of Beauty (London, 1878): 47, 62, 75, 88

Elizabeth Hawes
New York fashion designer and writer, labels Hawes-Harden and Elizabeth Hawes (1903–71)
Fashion is Spinach (New York, 1938): 21, 23, 42

Edith Head
Hollywood costume designer (1897–1981)
The Dress Doctor, E. Head and J. Ardmore (Surrey, 1959): 108

Mrs Millicent Hearst
Socialite and philanthropist wife of media tycoon Randolph (1882–1974)
Quoted in *Christian Dior: The Man Who Made the World Look New*, M. Pochna (New York, 1996): 35

Mrs Robert Henrey
The writer Madeleine Henrey who specialized in autobiography
This Feminine World (London, 1956): 70

Caroline Herrera
New York fashion designer (1939–)
Caroline Herrera: Portrait of a Fashion Icon, A. Katour (New York, 2004): 11, 45

Frances Hinchcliffe
Former V&A curator
Thirties Floral Fabrics (London, 1988): 51

T. H. Holding
Writer on tailoring (1844–1930)
Direct System of Ladies' Cutting (London, 1897): 113

Barbara Hulanicki
London fashion designer, label Biba (1936–)
From A to Biba (London, 2007): 34, 46, 125

Janey Ironside
Professor of fashion design, Royal College of Art
A Fashion Alphabet (London, 1968): 113

Stephen Jones
London milliner (1957–)
Couture in the Twenty-First Century, D. Bee (London, 2010): 59

Terry Jones
Editor of *i-D* magazine
Fashion Now, T. Jones and A. Mair (London, 2009): 109

Rei Kawakubo
Japanese fashion designer, label Comme des Garçons (1942–)
Comme des Garçons, Fashion Memoir, F. Grand (London, 1998): 32

Margaret Kornitzer
Writer on family life, adoption and women
The Modern Woman and Herself (London, 1932): 32, 124

Christian Lacroix
Parisian fashion designer of now defunct label Lacroix (1951–)
Pieces of a Pattern: Lacroix by Lacroix (London, 1992): 84
La Mode 1900–1999: Le siècle des créateurs, C. Seeling (Cologne, 2000): 17

Karl Lagerfeld
German designer and photographer, now based in Paris as head designer and creative director
for Chanel (1933–)
Quoted in Augustin, A., 'Les fashion secrets de Karl et Diane', French *Glamour*, March
2011: 125

Doris Langley-Moore
Fashion collector, curator and historian (1902–89)
Pleasure (London, 1953): 105, 120

James Laver
V&A curator and historian of fashion imagery
Taste and Fashion (London, 1945): 9, 12, 28, 33, 42, 77, 106, 121

Lucien Lelong
Parisian couturier (1889–1958)
Lucien Lelong, Jacqueline Demornex (London, 2008): 70

François Lesage
Head of the House of Lesage, a famous Parisian embroidery house now owned by Chanel
Chère Haute Couture, J. Samet (Paris, 2006): 39

Christian Louboutin
Parisian shoemaker, label Louboutin (1964–),
Declaration in Support of Acquired Distinctiveness, 14 March 2007: 105

Maison Martin Margiela
Belgian fashion designer, label Maison Martin Margiela (1957–)
Quoted in J. Kosuth Studio, 'Maison Martin Margiela', http://www.interviewmagazine.com: 73

Richard Martin
Associate curator, The Costume Institute collection, Metropolitan Museum of Art
Orientalism: Visions of the East in Western Dress (New York, 1995): 69

Gertrude Mason
Writer on making and adapting clothes
New Life for Old Clothes (London, 1942): 81 (both)

Claire McCardell
New York fashion designer, label Claire McCardell (1905–58)
Fashion is Our Business, B. Williams (London, 1948): 107
What Shall I Wear? (New York: 2009): 11, 13, 43, 75, 95

Alexander McQueen
London designer (1969–2010)
Quoted in SHOWstudio, http://showstudio.com/project/platos_atlantis#interview: 78

Valerie Mendes
Curator and fashion historian
Black in Fashion (London, 1999): 17

Suzy Menkes
Fashion writer and *International Herald Tribune* editor
International Herald Tribune, 20 December 2005: 105

E. Merriam
Writer on the fashion industry
Figleaf: The Business of Being in Fashion (Philadelphia, 1960): 16

Erdem Moralioğlu
London designer, label Erdem (1977–)
C. D'Souza in *Harper's Bazaar*, http://www.harpersbazaar.com/bazaar-blog/erdem-florals-spring-2011-collections: 48

Ira Morris
Designer and art editor
The Glass of Fashion (London, 1947): 28, 82, 114, 128

Grace Margaret Morton
Fashion professor and writer
The Arts of Costume and Personal Appearance (New York, 1943): 109

Kate Moss
British supermodel (1974–)
Quoted in interview with *Women's Wear Daily*, 2009: 34

Roland Mouret
Parisian fashion designer, labels Roland Mouret and RM by Roland Mouret (1962–)
Couture in the Twenty-First Century, D. Bee (London, 2010): 15

Jean Muir
London fashion designer, label Jean Muir (1928–95)
Leeds City Art Gallery, exhib. cat. (London, 1981): 32

Geoffrey Munn
Jewellery historian
Tiaras Past and Present (London, 2002), 112

'Myrene'
Pseudonym of anonymous beauty writer
The Lady Beauty Book, The Lady Magazine (London, 1900): 27

Paul Nystrom
Director of America's Retail Research Association, 1921–7 (1878–1969)
Economics of Fashion (New York, 1928): 93, 127

Todd Oldham
American fashion designer, label Todd Oldham (1961–)
Quoted in *Todd Oldham: Without Boundaries* (New York, 1997): 45

Betty Page
Writer on the fashion industry and etiquette
On Fair Vanity (London, 1954): 33, 47, 63, 83, 88, 91, 105

Jean Patou
Parisian fashion designer, label Jean Patou (1880–1936)
Patou, M. Etherington Smith (London, 1983): 73

Stephanie Pearl-McPhee
Writer on knitting (1968–)
At Knit's End (North Adams, MA, 2005): 71

Anna Piaggi
Italian fashion writer and style icon
Missonologia Electa (Milan, 1984): 25

Paul Poiret
Parisian fashion designer, label Poiret (1879–1944)
King of Fashion (London, 2009): 77

Emily Post
Writer on etiquette (1872–1960)
Etiquette (New York, 1924): 123
Copyright © 2004 by The Emily Post Institute, Inc. Reprinted by permission of HarperCollins
Publishers

Mrs Eric Pritchard
Journalist and writer
The Cult of Chiffon (London, 1902): 15, 21, 27, 34, 37, 47, 52, 59, 65, 75, 76, 78, 83, 91,
105, 106, 107, 111, 119

Mary Quant
London fashion designer, label Mary Quant (1934–)
Quant on Quant (London, 1966): 17, 25, 28, 31, 35, 128

Helena Rubenstein
Beauty scientist and entrepreneur (1872–1966)
My Life for Beauty (London, 1964): 87

Vita Sackville-West
Author, poet and gardener (1892–1962)
Portrait of a Marriage, N. Nicholson (Chicago, 1994): 114

Yves Saint Laurent
Algerian fashion designer who was based in Paris, label Yves Saint Laurent (1936–2008)
Yves Saint Laurent, Benaim (Paris, 2002): 27, 38, 93, 95, 108, 111, 115
Yves Saint Laurent (New York, 1983): 58, 85

Arnold Scaasi
American fashion designer, label Arnold Scaasi (1930–)
Scaasi: A Cut Above, B. Morris (New York, 1996): 59

Elsa Schiaparelli
Italian fashion designer who was based in Paris, label Elsa Schiparelli (1890–1973)
Shocking Life (London, 2007): 17, 19, 33, 94, 127

Anne Scott-James
Fashion writer, wrote for *Picture Post* (1913–2009)
Sketches from a Life (London, 1993): 51

Dame Edith Sitwell
British poet, writer and critic (1887–1964)
The Literary Companion to Fashion, C. McDowell (London, 1995): 37
Selected letters of Edith Sitwell, R. Greene ed. (London, 1997): 70

Carmel Snow
Journalist at American *Vogue* 1921–34, then editor of *Harper's Bazaar* 1934–58 (1887–1961)
The World of Carmel Snow (Maidenhead, 1961): 31, 38

Ginnette Spanier
Directrice of the House of Balmain
It Isn't All Mink (London, 1959): 23, 34, 47, 120

Margaret Story
Writer on fashion and etiquette
How to Dress Well (1924): 11, 41, 57, 75, 107, 119

Aage Thaarup
Danish milliner who worked in London, label Aage Thaarup (1906–87)
Heads and Tales (London, 1956): 83, 97

Mary Thomas
Writer on knitwear
Mary Thomas's Knitting Book (London, 1938): 70

Valentino
Full name: Valentino Garavani, Milanese fashion designer, label Valentino (1932–)
Valentino: Themes and Variations, P. Golbin (New York, 2008): 38
Valentino: Thirty Years of Magic, M-P Pelle (London, 1990): 48

Donatella Versace
Milanese fashion designer, label Versace (1955–)
Quoted in C. D'Souza,'The Odd Couple: Christopher Kane and Donatella Versace',
W magazine, http://www.wmagazine.com/fashion/2010/10/christopher_kane_donatella_
versace#ixzz1C8wRxkFI: 79

Gianni Versace
Milanese fashion designer, label Versace (1946–97)
The Art and Craft of Gianni Versace, C. Buss (London, 2002): 17

Madeleine Vionnet
Parisian fashion designer, label Vionnet (1876–1975)
Vionnet, B. Kirke (San Francisco, 1998): 15

Diana Vreeland
Curator and editor of *Harper's Bazaar* 1937–62 and American *Vogue* 1963–71 (1903–89)
Allure (Boston, 2002): 38, 112
DV (London, 1984): 26 (all quotes), 35, 56, 58
Inventive Clothes, 1909–1939 (London; New York, 1977): 45

Christina Walkley and Vanda Foster
Curators and dress historians
Crinolines and Crimping Irons (London, 1985): 73

Vivienne Westwood
London fashion designer, labels Vivienne Westwood Red Label, Gold Label, Anglomania
(1941–)
Quoted in *The Telegraph*, http://ethicalstyle.com/2008/10/vivienne-westwood-do-it-
yourself/: 120

Beryl Williams
Writer on American fashion
Fashion is Our Business (London, 1948): 13

Audrey Withers
Editor of British *Vogue* 1940–60 (1905–2001)
Lifespan (London, 1994): 63

Yohji Yamamoto
Japanese fashion designer based in Paris, label Yohji Yamamoto (1943–)
Yohji Yamamoto, F. Baudot (London, 1997): 45
Interview with Susannah Frankel, *The Independent on Sunday*, 21 November 2010: 11
Future Beauty: 30 Years of Japanese Fashion, A. Fukai et al (London, 2010): 17

Misc.

Berg Encyclopedia of World Dress and Fashion, volume 10 (Oxford, 2010): 76

Complete Etiquette for Ladies and Gentleman (London, 1900): 101

Dress Decoration and Ornament, Woman's Institute of Domestic Arts and Sciences Inc (London, 1925): 100

Enquire Within Upon Everything (London,1894): 57

The Independent, 'Sex and the City', 29 July 2002: 78

Jaeger's Natural History, Jaeger Publishing House (London, 1930s): 21

The Ladies Realm, December 1906: 111

The Lancet, quoted by Stella Mary Newton in *Health, Art & Reason* (London,1879): 113

Laundering and Dry Cleaning, Women's Institute (London, 1925): 63, 74

Manners and Rules of Good Society or Solecisms to be Avoided (London, 1893): 39, 88

Manners of Modern Society (London, 1877): 39, 88, 99, 101, 127

Modern Etiquette in Public and Private (London, 1891): 55 (both), 62, 79, 87

Oxford English Dictionary (Oxford, 1991): 42, 108

Time, 29 June 1962: 76

Vogue's Book of Etiquette and Good Manners (New York, 1969): 62, 87, 101